Five Steps to Strengthen Ethics in Organizations and Individuals

Five Steps to Strengthen Ethics in Organizations and Individuals draws on research and history to present effective tools to strengthen organizational ethics. Focusing on key topics such as the planning fallacy, moral disengagement, moral courage, the illusion of ethical superiority, confirmation bias, groupthink, whistleblowers, mindfulness and mindlessness, making authentic apologies, and more, this book discusses specific positive actions that get results and avoid common pitfalls. Research findings and examples from organizations—including missteps by the Veterans Administration, Penn State University, the APA, General Motors, Enron, and Wells Fargo—inform the strategies this book presents and highlight lessons in organizational ethics. Scholars, researchers, professionals, administrators, students, and others interested in organizational studies and ethics will find this unique book essential in training and practice.

Kenneth S. Pope is a licensed psychologist and Fellow of the Association for Psychological Science. He served as chair of the Ethics Committees of the American Board of Professional Psychology and the American Psychological Association.

"We expect the very best from Pope, and this must-read ethics guide delivers. Scrupulously researched, this landmark contribution will be indispensable to all organizations and individuals committed to ethical decision-making and behavior, and to courses on ethics and organizational psychology."

—**Martin Drapeau**, Professor of Counselling Psychology and Psychiatry, McGill University; Editor in Chief of *Canadian Psychology/Psychologie Canadienne*

"Ken Pope has done it again. Here is a timely, clear, well-researched, action-oriented book replete with organizational examples which is designed to get organizations and individuals to fortify their ethical stance. This book is essential reading for those studying or working in organizations."

—**Judie Alpert**, Professor of Applied Psychology, New York University

"Once again, Ken Pope shows courageous leadership and guides by stellar example. Using research findings and examples from well-known ethical missteps from major American organization icons, Pope shows how and why we all can strengthen ethics at work."

—**Joan M. Cook**, Associate Professor, Yale School of Medicine; Lecturer, Yale School of Management

"This engaging new book by Ken Pope is essential reading for everyone who believes all organizations—non-profit and for-profit—should model idealized ethical standards, top-down from the CEO and bottom-up from the kitchen and mail room staff. Honoring what is best in our human nature creates a new generation of Everyday Heroes."

—**Phil Zimbardo**, Professor Emeritus of Psychology, Stanford University; Author of *The Lucifer Effect*; President of The Heroic Imagination Project

Five Steps to Strengthen Ethics in Organizations and Individuals

Effective Strategies Informed by Research and History

Kenneth S. Pope

Routledge
Taylor & Francis Group

LONDON AND NEW YORK

First published 2018 by Routledge

2 Park Square, Milton Park, Abingdon, Oxfordshire OX14 4RN
52 Vanderbilt Avenue, New York, NY 10017

Routledge is an imprint of the Taylor & Francis Group, an informa business

First issued in paperback 2019

Copyright © 2018 Taylor & Francis

Library of Congress Cataloging-in-Publication Data
A catalog record for this book has been requested

ISBN: 978-1-138-72476-1 (hbk)
ISBN: 978-0-367-34886-1 (pbk)

Typeset in Times New Roman
by Apex Covantage, LLC

For Karen, the love of my life, who every day
makes me feel that I am the luckiest person who
ever lived.

Contents

About the Author

Kenneth S. Pope, Ph.D., ABPP is a licensed psychologist who received his Diplomate from the American Board of Professional Psychology. A Fellow of the Association for Psychological Science (APS), he served as chair of the Ethics Committees of the American Board of Professional Psychology and the American Psychological Association (APA). He received the APA Award for Distinguished Contributions to Public Service, the APA Division 12 Award for Distinguished Professional Contributions to Clinical Psychology, the Canadian Psychological Association's John C. Service Member of the Year Award, and the Ontario Psychological Association's Barbara Wand Award for significant contribution to excellence in professional ethics and standards. His most recent publications are "The Code Not Taken: The Path From Guild Ethics to Torture and Our Continuing Choices—Award Address" in *Canadian Psychology/psychologie Canadienne* and *Ethics in Psychotherapy and Counseling: A Practical Guide, 5th Edition* (with co-author Melba Vasquez).

OK, that's the formalistic version, written in the traditional but bizarre third person, as if someone else were writing it. (How many people do you know who talk about themselves in the third person?) Enough of that. Let me try a different way.

Going to hear Dr. Martin Luther King, Jr., and the community organizer Saul Alinsky changed my life forever. Their words shook me awake, wouldn't let go.

By the time I graduated from college, their words had convinced me to delay a fellowship to study literature so that I could learn community organizing and try to make a difference. I worked in an inner-city area of severe poverty during the late 1960s and early 1970s. For the first time in my life, I lived where there were no neighbors of my own race.

Those years showed me how poverty, unmet basic needs, and injustice can assault individual lives. I also witnessed the power of people working together to bring about profound change within organizations.

A crucial lesson began one day in a cafe where the community gathered. A deacon in a church whose roots reached back to the days before the Civil War invited me to visit the church that Sunday.

I entered the church that weekend and found a seat at the back, looking forward to the minister's sermon. When the time came for the sermon, the minister walked up to the pulpit, looked out at us, and began, "We are most pleased that our neighbor, Mr. Ken Pope, agreed to visit us today, and we look forward to his sermon." This taught me not to assume that my understandings are always shared by others— and that life often calls us to do more than just show up.

After my years living in that community, I began the delayed fellowship to study literature at Harvard. But the years between college and graduate school had changed me. When I received an M.A. at the end of the year, I did not want to continue studies in that field. I explained my change of heart, expecting to be shown the door. But my advisors surprised me. They told me I could continue to study, taking whatever courses I found interesting in any fields. Some courses I took the next year were in psychology and they felt like my home. I'll always be thankful to the university for their kindness in allowing me to delay my fellowship, in letting me take courses in diverse fields, and in the professors' generosity with their time and support. Because Harvard lacked a clinical psychology program, I transferred to Yale for my clinical psychology doctorate.

What happened in these early years has kept happening throughout my life: Fellow students, colleagues, patients, and others have made me realize that whatever beliefs I held at any given time could be rethought, that I needed to consider new perspectives, new possibilities, new ways of finding, creating, and using resources.

One example: Our faculty-intern discussions followed a predictable pattern: Asked to present a case, each of us interns would choose to describe that week's version of "my toughest case," making clear what tough challenges we faced and how brilliant our insights and interventions. Midyear, an intern broke the pattern: "I feel awful this week. The situation was not that difficult but I made some bad mistakes, and ended up having to hospitalize the patient. I need help figuring out what's going on with this patient, why I did what I did, and how I can do things differently." Her honesty, courage, integrity, and clear concern for the person she wanted to help woke us from our complacent habits of thinking and feeling. We confronted how we approached learning and how we treated each other. We talked about how fear, envy, and competitiveness affected who we were, how we thought, what we did. One person had changed our community.

In my early years as a licensed psychologist, I served as clinical director of a nonprofit hospital and community mental health center. My prior experiences with community organizations led me to focus on the ability of the staff, the Board of Directors, and the surrounding community to work together identifying needs and creating ways to meet those needs. Working together, the diverse individuals in that array of groups created home-bound psychological services, a 24-hour crisis service, legal services for people who are poor or homeless, a program for people whose primary language is Spanish, and group homes allowing people who are mentally disabled to live independently. What the people in these groups accomplished showed again and again the decisive role that each can play in the lives of others, the ways we can awaken each other to new perspectives and possibilities, the roles each of us can play in strengthening ethics in organizations and the people within those organizations, and how people working together can bring about change.

Teaching the occasional undergraduate course in the UCLA psychology department, supervising therapy in the UCLA Psychology Clinic, chairing the ethics committees of the American Psychological Association (APA) and the American Board of Professional Psychology (ABPP), becoming a charter member and later Fellow of what is now the Association of Psychological Science, and other experiences in those early years kept reminding me of the need to keep rethinking what I think I know and my ways of working, to ask "What if I'm wrong about this?", "Is there a better way to understand this?", "What else could I do that might be more effective?"

In decades that followed, the themes of my work, touched on above, continue, even as they continue to take on new forms.

One question I've struggled with is: How can psychologists have better access to relevant information without it adding to their time-restraints and financial burden?

Two decades ago, I started a Psychology News List via email, free and open to all. I wanted to make it a little easier—especially for those in isolated areas or those who lack easy access to the relevant materials—to keep up with the new research, changing legal standards, controversial topics, and other trends that affect our work. Each day I send out 6–10 items, most of them excerpts from new and in-press articles from psychology and other scientific and professional journals, psychology-related articles from that day's newspapers, new court decisions affecting psychology, job announcements, and referral requests sent to me by list members. Although not a discussion list and now quite large, it has become a supportive community. From time to time members ask me to circulate a request for information or suggestions for dealing with an aging parent, a family emergency, a clinical or forensic issue, or a business-related problem with their practice—almost all write me later to tell me how supported they felt to receive so many personal responses.

Every year I've sent a question to the list: Between the Canadian and U.S. Thanksgivings, I ask what they are especially thankful for that year. When I circulate a compilation of all the responses, members tell me how much the process makes them feel less alone and more connected to others.

Another way we can make information more accessible is through websites that provide articles and other resources without making access contingent on subscriptions, memberships, fees, or other restrictions. Two of mine are "Articles, Research, & Resources in Psychology" at http://kspope.com and "Accessibility & Disability Information & Resources in Psychology Training & Practice" at http://kpope.com.

For 29 years APA was my professional home. As chair of the APA Ethics Committee and a Fellow of 9 APA Divisions, I worked with many people who became close friends and gave so much to my professional and personal life. I was honored to receive the APA Award for Distinguished Contributions to Public Service "for rigorous empirical research, landmark articles and books, courageous leadership, fostering the careers of others, and making services available to those with no means to pay"; the Division 12 Award for Distinguished Professional Contributions to Clinical Psychology; the Division 42 Award for Mentoring; and other forms of recognition.

In 2008, with great regret and sadness I resigned from the APA. My respect and affection for the members made this a hard and reluctant step. I respectfully disagreed with decisive changes that APA made in its ethical stance after 9/11. In my view, those changes moved APA far from its ethical foundation, historic traditions, and basic values, and beyond what I could in good conscience support with my membership. 9/11 cast all of us into a tangle of complex issues, dangerous realities, and hard choices. My decision to resign from APA reflected my effort to judge what was right for me. I respect those who saw things differently, held other beliefs, took other paths.

We can each give so much to each other and to organizations. Sometimes just a word or gesture helps someone to keep going, overcome a baffling obstacle, or see new vistas. An example: During that second year at Harvard I signed up for an advanced course in the med school. The first day I was already lost. The professor kept asking if we saw various structures in our microscopes. Everyone nodded yes, but I had no idea what he was talking about. I was too embarrassed to admit I couldn't see any of them. Finally I raised my hand and confessed. He looked at me a long time, then came down the aisle, put his hand on my back, leaned down to the floor, and plugged in my electronic microscope. Sometimes that's all it takes.

Acknowledgments and Copyrights

First and foremost I wish to thank Christina Chronister, Editor at Routledge of the Taylor & Francis Group, for reaching out to me with an invitation to write this book. Without her wonderful encouragement and support, this book never would have seen the light of day.

I owe a tremendous debt of gratitude for the thoughtful, skilled work of everyone at Taylor & Francis who had a hand in making this project work: Christina Chronister, Julie Toich, Denise File, Carmel A. Huestis, and Katie McIlvanie.

I greatly appreciate being allowed to both quote and adapt material from a segment of my article "The Code Not Taken: The Path From Guild Ethics to Torture and Our Continuing Choices—John C. Service Member of the Year Award," which was published in *Canadian Psychology/psychologie Canadienne*. Copyright © 2016 Canadian Psychological Association. This material, which I've included in Chapter 2, is used with permission. No further reproduction or distribution is permitted without written permission from the American Psychological Association.

I also greatly appreciate being allowed to both quote and adapt material from my article "Steps to Strengthen Ethics in Organizations: Research Findings, Ethics Placebos, and What Works" in *Journal of Trauma & Dissociation*. Material from this article was used by permission of Taylor & Francis LLC (www.tandfonline.com).

Heartfelt thanks to psychologists Ray Arsenault, Kate Hays, and Loralai Lawson, who took time to read the manuscript and offer extremely valuable suggestions for improving it.

And thanks to Karen Olio, to whom I dedicate this book, for her unfailing support, insightful editorial comments, and good cheer throughout the process.

1   Understanding the Challenges and Seizing the Opportunities to Strengthen Ethics in Organizations and Individuals

Each of us, no matter our place inside or outside an organization, can work at strengthening its ethics. Research and history give us tools that can raise our odds of success. What is baffling—or perhaps not, given human nature—is that these tools tend to rust away unused, as the studies and examples in this book show in vivid, sometimes gruesome and fatal detail.

What can we learn from research and history about strengthening ethics in organizations and the individuals making up those organizations? This book draws together relevant research and examples that show us practical steps we can take to make a difference.

The challenge of changing an organization's ethical awareness, character, commitment, and behavior can strike us as a heavy lift or just downright impossible. Inching the organization toward ethical excellence, dragging it out of ethical scandal, or just overcoming organizational inertia can seem far out of reach.

Organizations With Strong Ethics

How in the world do they do it, those organizations that build up ethical strength? We see them standing fast against pressure, temptation, and rationalization. We see them do the right thing when they come to ethical crossroads, slippery slopes, and minefields. They can surprise the cynics with their deep and unwavering ethical commitment. An ethic of honesty, humanity, fairness, and responsibility runs through the organization. Members of the organization treat each other and outsiders with respect. They earn and deserve our trust. They take great care not to betray that trust.

And yet those organizations that radiate ethical strength are made up of people like you and me, people who know firsthand feelings like envy, greed, entitlement, smugness, temptation to lie (but for a good cause! And just this once!) or cheat (but if you knew the circumstances, you'd understand! You'd do the same! Who wouldn't?), and all the other human traits we share but rarely advertise. Just like us, they are not free of bias and blind spots.

Organizations With Weak or Cosmetic Ethics

People like us also make up the organizations plagued with ethical weakness or inconsistency. We know some of the high-profile offenders from newspaper headlines and court cases described later in this book. Others give us clear but easy-to-miss hints such as repeatedly charging us incorrect amounts or giving us incorrect change, always conveniently in favor of the organization. They are often full of phony smiles, indifference, or rudeness, despite constantly assuring us of how much they value us as employees, members, customers, clients, patients, volunteers, or supporters. But some offenders—including examples described later—show an uncanny genius at masking ethical weakness and betrayals of trust. The ethical make-up of these organizations is all made up and applied like a cosmetic to cover what lies beneath.

Some violate ethical standards with premeditation; others make a practice of never meditating on ethics. Some lapse into ethical numbness, operate in an ethical haze, or settle for ethical mediocrity or what strikes them (but perhaps not others) as "good enough" ethics. Many reveal a special gift for shrugging off ethics violations. All are quick to deny any ethical impropriety, to come up with excuses, and to change the subject. For them, any mention of ethical commitment is hyperbole.

Ethics Placebos, Zombie Ethics, Magic Bullets, and the Usual Suspects

A search for ways to strengthen ethics in an organization often ends quickly by rounding up the usual suspects. These are the tools, methods, and approaches that are all too familiar to us. They *seem* like they can be counted on. We grab them quickly, in part because they are popular—after all, why would so many people be using them if they didn't work? Too often they turn out to be, as research and history warn us, illusory interventions, promising much, delivering little if anything, aside from the guise of change.

Some popular interventions are little more than ethics placebos, leaving us feeling better and perhaps even satisfied with our efforts but leaving the organization no stronger in its ethics than before we began. We scurry in a flurry of busy-ness, releasing public statements, forming committees, studying the issues, circulating drafts, issuing reports, making plans, getting rid of bad apples, restaffing and reorganizing re: ethics.

Some people inside or outside the organization probably have an idea where all this massive movement will wind up, because they know the organization. They know its history, character, purpose, power-holders, and the carrots and sticks, both internal and external, that it responds to. They can anticipate that the organization—perhaps unintentionally—will emerge from this whirlwind of activity with pretty much the same ethical climate and behavior that it had before. Hanna wrote: "All organizations are perfectly designed to get the results they get" (1988, p. 36; see also Mitchell, 2015, for the evolution of this quotation and its corollary, "Every system is perfectly designed to get the results it gets."). Ethics placebos, for all their good intentions and feel-good quality, fail to address the ways (and reasons) the organization was designed to produce its current ethical awareness, character, commitment, and behavior. They fail to direct our awareness and action to why and how the organization was designed to create its current ethical status and how that design lays the groundwork for, invites, and promotes its re-creation.

If ethics placebos tend to be feel-good interventions, zombie ethics feel bad and can be frightening, at least to those who are not at the top. Zombie ethics mistake rules, orders, and decrees imposed by those in authority, for ethical awareness and informed, thoughtful decision-making based in personal responsibility and accountability (Pope & Vasquez, 2016). The rules, orders, and decrees, however elegant and eloquent, feel to many in the organization like something mashed down on their heads (or crammed down their throats) from on high, something imposed on them (and experienced as an unwanted imposition) by well-meaning (maybe) out-of-touch leaders or clueless committees. They have a deadening effect.

Particularly when caught in a scandal or needing a public relations boost, organizations look for that wonderful one magic bullet that puts to eternal rest all ethical problems, questions, concerns, and bad publicity. One organization faced down skeptics around the world by pointing with pride to a remarkably thoughtful, detailed, and comprehensive ethics code that every employee read and signed before beginning work. The code was widely praised and soon adapted and adopted by a variety of other businesses. Later, as described in Chapter 3, the company made headlines for scamming billions of dollars.

Chapter 3 reviews research on the factors that make ethics codes effective, and discusses ways to create and revise ethics codes so that they are not simply cosmetic public relations or failed attempts to find a magic bullet.

Other organizations place their faith in another magical cure-all: emphasizing ethics explicitly in their policies, documents, and public statements. This apparently sensible strategy seemingly makes sure that nothing escapes ethical examination. As the longed-for one magic bullet, it misses the mark and fails miserably. Loughran, McDonald, and Yun (2008) examined the occurrence of ethics-related language in companies' annual reports submitted as required to the U.S. Securities and Exchange Commission over a 12-year period. These reports include not only comprehensive information about the company's financial performance but also about its origins, history, structure, and so on. They found that "firms using ethics-related terms are more likely to be 'sin' stocks, are more likely to be the object of class action lawsuits, and are more likely to score poorly on measures of corporate governance" (p. 39). Organizations scoring lowest in governance had a particular tendency to assert that they upheld the highest ethical standards. These forceful assertions of virtue reflect Ralph Waldo Emerson's 1860 comment about an adventurer: "the louder he talked of his honor, the faster we counted our spoons" (2007, VI. Worship, para. 9).

Plenty of Opportunities: Examples

We live in an age rich with opportunities to make organizational ethics stronger. Striking betrayals of ethics and trust grab headlines:

- In 2014, General Motors (GM) admitted that since 2001 it had hidden a potentially fatal design defect. GM engineers, investigators, and lawyers knew, but the company decided that recalling cars would cost too much. Instead, they kept the flaw secret for more than a decade. They kept selling risky cars while the deaths related to the problem climbed to at least 124 according to GM's own admission (its count has been contested as low) and injuries—including brain damage, amputation, and quadriplegia—surged (Bennett, 2014; Consumer Reports, 2014; General Motors, 2016; Viscusi, 2015; Young, 2014, 2015a, 2015b). This design flaw that was causing so many deaths and such catastrophic injuries was widely known in the company. National Highway Traffic and Safety Administration acting chief

David Friedman stated when fining GM: "GM engineers knew about the defect. GM investigators knew about the defect. GM lawyers knew about the defect. But GM did not act to protect Americans from that defect" (Fletcher, 2014).

- Famous for its football program's integrity, Penn State covered up child abuse for years, allowing the abuser to continue committing crimes. The report commissioned by the university stressed "the total and consistent disregard by the most senior leaders at Penn State for the safety and welfare of Sandusky's child victims" (Freeh, Sporken, & Sullivan, LLP, 2012, p. 14; see also Tracy, 2016). Several ways the school responded to this scandal sparked widespread controversy and criticism. For example, a judge awarded a whistleblower a total of $12,000,000, finding that Penn State had not only de facto fired him in retaliation but also subjected him to defamation, humiliation, and legal misrepresentation, making him persona non grata in the world of football (Ingram, 2016; Thompson, 2016). Brennan wrote: "For nearly five years now, school officials have consistently made the worst public-relations decisions about the scandal and its aftermath, ensuring that instead of making it go away, they've kept it front and center in our national consciousness (2016; see also Jaschik, 2016). In March 2017, a Penn State trustee's email about "Running out of sympathy for 35 yr old, so-called victims" was the focus of renewed controversy and criticism (Stripling, 2017).
- In 1979 California finally repealed its "compulsory sterilization laws [that] targeted minorities, the poor, the disabled, the mentally ill and criminals" (Johnson, 2014) and had allowed the state to force sterilization on more than 20,000 children and adults in state-run institutions from 1909 to 1979 (Reverby, 2017; Stern, 2015; Stern et al., 2017; Wellerstein, 2011). (Of the more than 900 survivors, not one has been compensated by the state at the time I write this book; the governor offered an apology instead of compensation.) Although the law allowing these sterilizations was repealed, the practice continued. The California State Auditor (2014) reported that between 2005 and 2013 the state prison system had continued to sterilize some female prisoners, violating the law, the right to informed consent, and the safeguards intended to make sure prisons did not illegally sterilize girls and women.
- Many Veterans Administration (VA) executives pocketed hefty bonuses for making sure that sick veterans got prompt care, but it was a con. Hospitals reported that they were giving all veterans

prompt care when needed. Instead, they were secretly shunting tens of thousands of veterans to secret waiting lists where they languished without care for months, some dying without care (Bronstein & Griffin, 2014; Daly & Tang, 2014; Hoyer & Zoroya, 2014; Oppel & Shear, 2014; VA Office of the Inspector General, 2014; Wagner, 2014). At the time I write this book, reforms have not eliminated these problems and provided prompt care (Steele, 2017; Theobold, 2016; Wagner, 2016).

Plenty of Opportunities: Studies

Studies suggest that many organizations violate basic ethics and betray our trust:

- A Gallup survey found:

    Americans' confidence in the nation's major institutions continues to lag below historical averages, with two institutions—newspapers and organized religion—dropping to record lows this year. The overall average of Americans expressing "a great deal" or "quite a lot" of confidence in institutions is below 33% for the third straight year.

    (Norman, 2016)

- The *2017 Edelman Trust Barometer: Global Annual Study* (Edelman, 2017; see also Harrington, 2017) found "the largest-ever drop in trust across the institutions of government, business, media and NGOs." It was the first time this annual survey of over 33,000 people in 28 countries showed a drop in trust in all 4 institutions. In two-thirds of the countries, less than half the people trusted these institutions "to do what is right." The findings were so grim that the authors termed it an "implosion of trust."
- Huberts (2014) noted that almost half of U.S. workers reported seeing one or more acts of wrongdoing (e.g., accepting kickbacks or bribes, offering bribes to public officials, lying to outside stakeholders, environmental violations) on the job within the past year.
- A study of full-time U.S. workers found that almost three fourths reported encountering ethical lapses at work, with one tenth believing that the lapse could create a scandal or business disruption (LRN, 2007; see also McCarthy, 2016).
- The 28th Annual Retail Theft Survey found that one in every 38 employees was apprehended for stealing from the employer,

representing an increase in employee theft for 9 of the past 10 years (Jack L. Hayes International, 2016).

- According to Stevens (2013), "Confidence in the ethics of the U.S. business executive remains fairly low on the Gallup Poll surveys and the U.S. has declined on the CPI (Consumer Price Index) and Edelman Trust Barometer" (p. 361).
- In the introduction to a special issue of the *Journal of Law, Medicine & Ethics*, Rodwin (2013) wrote that "today, the goals of pharmaceutical policy and medical practice are often undermined due to institutional corruption—that is, widespread or systemic practices, usually legal, that undermine an institution's objectives or integrity" (p. 544). Elliott (2014) noted that in 2010 the pharmaceutical industry eclipsed the defense industry as the biggest defrauder of the U.S. government.
- A study found that campus judicial systems tend to give light sentences (e.g., writing an essay) for serious violations such as sexual assaults, physical attacks causing serious injuries, robberies, and other violent felonies, leaving many students reporting that "the system is unfair" and that the campus "has betrayed them" (Binkley, Wagner, Riepenhoff, & Gregory, 2014).
- Twenge, Campbell, and Carter (2014) reported that "confidence in institutions . . . reached historic lows among Americans" (p. 1920). They emphasized that the loss of trust and confidence extends across a wide array of institutions: "The trend is not limited to distrust in government; the declines also appear in Americans' confidence in institutions unconnected to the government, such as medicine, religion, the news media, and TV" (p. 1921).

The Perfect Storm

This book suggests 5 practical steps, informed by history and research, to take advantage of opportunities to strengthen ethics in organizations and the people that make up those organizations. The steps are illustrated through what happened when a historic and highly respected organization ran into a perfect storm of factors, resulting in an ethics scandal spotlighted in international headlines, a formal apology for creating an ethical stain on the profession, and a pledge to reset its moral compass. The next chapter will provide a brief, documented account of how the organization stumbled and then recovered its footing, followed by chapters describing each of the 5 steps.

References

Bennett, J. (2014, March 12). GM now says it detected ignition switch problem back in 2001. *Wall Street Journal*. Retrieved from http://on.wsj.com/2iQE0cu

Binkley, C., Wagner, M., Riepenhoff, J., & Gregory, S. (2014, November 23). College disciplinary boards impose slight penalties for serious crimes. *Columbus Dispatch*. Retrieved from www.dispatch.com/content/stories/local/2014/11/23/campus-injustice.html

Brennan, C. (2016, September 14). What is Penn State thinking in honoring Joe Paterno? *USA Today*. Retrieved from http://usat.ly/2i1bTpG

Bronstein, S., & Griffin, D. (2014, April 23). A fatal wait: Veterans languish and die on a VA hospital's secret list. *CNN*. Retrieved from http://bit.ly/1tLPRG9

California State Auditor. (2014, June). *Sterilization of female inmates: Some inmates were sterilized unlawfully, and safeguards designed to limit occurrences of the procedure failed.* Retrieved from www.auditor.ca.gov/pdfs/reports/2013-120.pdf

Consumer Reports. (2014, March). *GM recall raises concerns about warning systems for auto safety.* Retrieved from the Consumer Reports website: http://consumerreports.org/cro/2014/03/gm-recall-raises-concerns-about-warning-systems-for-auto-safety/index.htm

Daly, M., & Tang, T. (2014, June 6). VA chief: 18 vets left off waiting list have died. *Associated Press*. Retrieved from http://bigstory.ap.org/article/senate-moves-toward-voteva-health-care

Edelman. (2017). *2017 Edelman trust barometer: Global annual study.* Atlanta, GA: Edelman.

Elliott, C. (2014). Relationships between physicians and Pharma: Why physicians should not accept money from the pharmaceutical industry. *Neurology: Clinical Practice, 4*(2), 164–167.

Emerson, R. W. (2007). *Conduct of life* [Kindle for the Mac version]. New York, NY: Cosimo. (Originally published in 1860.) Retrieved from Amazon.com

Fletcher, M. (2014, June 5). GM releases results of ignition-switch probe. *Washington Post*. Retrieved from http://wapo.st/2jcpGau

Freeh, Sporken, & Sullivan, LLP. (2012, July 12). *Report of the special investigative counsel regarding the actions of the Pennsylvania State University related to the child sexual abuse committed by Gerald A. Sandusky.* Retrieved from http://bit.ly/2iYYtc4

General Motors Company. (2016, February 3). *10K annual report to the United States securities and exchange commission.* Detroit: Author. Retrieved from http://bit.ly/2iMHjyS

Hanna, D. P. (1988). *Designing organizations for high performance.* Indianapolis, IN: FT Press.

Harrington, M. (2017). Survey: People's trust has declined in business, media, government, and NGOs. *Harvard Business Review*. Retrieved from https://hbr.org/2017/01/survey-peoples-trust-has-declined-in-business-media-government-and-ngos

Hoyer, M., & Zoroya, G. (2014, July 4). VA bonuses went to officials at delay-prone hospitals. *USA Today*. Retrieved from http://bit.ly/1owQJLP

Huberts, L. (2014). *Integrity of governance: What it is, what we know, what is done and where to go*. New York, NY: Palgrave Macmillan.

Ingram, D. (2016, November 30). Award for Penn State whistleblower in Sandusky scandal rises to $12 million. *Reuters*. Retrieved from http://reut.rs/2hYwHjf

Jack L. Hayes International. (2016, June). *Apprehension of shoplifters and dishonest employees has increased in 9 of the past 10 years, according to Jack L. Hayes International's 28th Annual Retail Theft Survey*. [Press release]. Retrieved from http://bit.ly/2jlCFHf

Jaschik, S. (2016, September 2). Outrage on Penn State Plan to Honor Paterno. *Inside Higher Education*.

Johnson, C. (2014, September 26). California bans coerced sterilization of female inmates. *Center for Investigative Reporting*. Retrieved from http://bit.ly/2hZh863

Loughran, T., McDonald, B., & Yun, H. (2008). A wolf in sheep's clothing: The use of ethics-related terms in 10-k reports. *Journal of Business Ethics, 89*(1), 39–49.

LRN. (2007). *LRN ethics study: Workplace productivity: A report on how ethical lapses and questionable behaviors distract U.S. workers*. Los Angeles, CA: LRN.

McCarthy, J. (2016, May 25). *Americans remain pessimistic about state of moral values*. Washington, DC: Gallup. Retrieved from http://bit.ly/1PfSUyW

Mitchell, K. (2015, August 21). Like magic? ("Every system is perfectly designed . . ."). *Institute of Healthcare Improvement Newsletter*. Retrieved from http://bit.ly/2iM9oGa

Norman, J. (2016, June 13). *Americans' confidence in institutions stays low*. Gallup Organization. Retrieved from http://www.gallup.com/poll/192581/americans-confidence-institutions-stays-low.aspx

Oppel, R. A., & Shear, M. D. (2014, May 29). Severe report finds V.A. hid waiting lists at hospitals. *New York Times*, p. A1.

Pope, K. S., & Vasquez, M. J. (2016). *Ethics in psychotherapy and counseling: A practical guide* (5th ed.). [Kindle for the Mac version]. New York, NY: John Wiley & Sons.

Reverby, S. M. (2017). Historical misfeasance: Immorality to justice in public health. *American Journal of Public Health, 107*(1), 14–15.

Rodwin, M. A. (2013). Introduction: Institutional corruption and the pharmaceutical policy. *Journal of Law, Medicine & Ethics, 41*, 544–552.

Steele, J. (2017, January 2). 4 biggest issues facing next Veterans Affairs secretary. *San Diego Union Tribune*. Retrieved from http://bit.ly/2jcIUgj

Stern, A. M. (2015). *Eugenic nation: Faults and frontiers of better breeding in modern America*. Berkeley, CA: University of California Press.

Stern, A. M., Novak, N. L., Lira, N., O'Connor, K., Harlow, S., & Kardia, S. (2017). California's sterilization survivors: An estimate and call for redress. *American Journal of Public Health, 107*(1), 50–54.

Stevens, B. (2013). How ethical are US business executives? A study of perceptions. *Journal of Business Ethics, 117*(2), 361–369.

Stripling, J. (2017, March 30). Seeking closure in verdict, Penn State finds more discord. *Chronicle of Higher Education*. Retrieved from http://bit.ly/2oS10eH

Theobold, B. (2016, October 28). More bonuses for VA employees despite ongoing problems at the agency. *USA Today*. Retrieved from http://bit.ly/2f1Efh0

Thompson, C. (2016, November 30). Judge rules against Penn State on Mike McQueary whistleblower claim; $5 million in additional damages ordered. *PENN Live*. Retrieved from www.pennlive.com/news/2016/11/judge_rules_against_penn_state.html

Tracy, M. (2016, July 12). Joe Paterno knew of Sandusky abuse in 1976, according to court testimony. *New York Times*. Retrieved from http://nyti.ms/2hZblxu

Twenge, J. M., Campbell, W. K., & Carter, N. T. (2014). Declines in trust in others and confidence in institutions among American adults and late adolescents, 1972–2012. *Psychological Science, 25*, 1914–1923.

VA Office of the Inspector General. (2014, May 28). *Veterans health administration—Interim report—Review of patient wait times, scheduling practices, and alleged patient deaths at the Phoenix Health Care System*. Retrieved from www.va.gov/oig/pubs/VAOIG-14-02603-178.pdf

Viscusi, W. K. (2015, May 14–26). Pricing lives for corporate risk decisions. *Vanderbilt Law Review*.

Wagner, D. (2014, June 9). VA scandal audit: 120,000 veterans experience long waits for care: Audit shows delayed care at VA facilities across U.S. *Arizona Republic*.

Wagner, D. (2016, October 4). Inspectors rip Phoenix VA hospital again for poor service. *Arizona Republic*. Retrieved from http://bit.ly/2cQHBoI

Wellerstein, A. (2011). States of eugenics: Institutions and practices in compulsory sterilization in California. In S. Jasanoff (Ed.), *Reframing rights: Bioconstitutionalism in the genetic age* (pp. 29–58). Cambridge, MA: MIT Press.

Young, A. (2014, June 2). GM ignition switch recall: What to expect from Valukas report. *International Business Times*. Retrieved from http://www.investing.com/news/stock-market-news/gm-ignition-switch-recall:-what-to-expect-from-valukas-report-287350

Young, A. (2015a, September 9). General Motors ignition switch flaw death toll rises to 169 following personal injury settlement. *International Business Times*. Retrieved from http://bit.ly/2jcczGu

Young, A. (2015b, May 5). GM could be held criminally liable for ignition switch flaw and pay a record penalty for not disclosing the problem sooner. *International Business Times*. Retrieved from http://bit.ly/2jcg67x

2 A Remarkable Organization Runs Into Trouble

How could it ever wind up like this? A remarkable organization—one that had earned so much respect and influence since its founding in 1892, had pioneered a remarkable new method for creating its first ethics code, had emphasized ethics throughout the organization—found itself confronting a major ethics scandal.

The scandal broke open with such force that the revelations led the American Psychological Association (APA) to formally "apologize for this stain on our collective integrity" (McDaniel & Kaslow, 2015c; see also 2015b) and to "acknowledge that that these events have cast a pall on psychology and psychologists in all countries, with the potential to negatively affect perceptions of the integrity of our discipline worldwide" (McDaniel & Kaslow, 2015b). The APA president and president-elect described the steps for "resetting our moral compass" (McDaniel & Kaslow, 2015a; see also Aldhaus, 2015, and Wilhelm, 2015). It was the kind of ethics scandal that no organization ever wants to face, a scandal that triggered investigations by newspaper reporters, congressional committees, human rights organizations, and a former federal prosecutor hired by APA.

The scandal holds useful lessons for strengthening ethics in organizations and individuals, for steering clear of missteps toward trouble, and for recovering from ethical stumbles. These lessons show us constructive steps that draw on research and history. They also form the structure for the chapters that follow, each devoted to one of these 5 steps. But first, it is useful to put what happened within APA in context.

Attacks Forcing Quick Decisions Based on Incomplete Information

The unprecedented attacks on U.S. civilians on 9/11 forced U.S. citizens and their leaders to make hard choices without knowing what threats lay ahead. To find out more about those threats, the government interrogated detainees at Camps Delta, Iguana, and X-Ray at Guantánamo Bay Naval Base, the Detention Centre at Bagram Airbase in Afghanistan, Abu Ghraib Prison in Iraq, and similar settings.

APA strongly supported the value of these interrogations and the need for psychologists to be involved. It explained to the U.S. Senate Select Committee on Intelligence that "conducting an interrogation is inherently a psychological endeavor. . . . Psychology is central to this process. . . . Psychologists have valuable contributions to make toward . . . protecting our nation's security through interrogation processes" (American Psychological Association, 2007b).

Psychologists would not only ensure that interrogations were effective in getting accurate and actionable intelligence but also ensure that *all interrogations* they participated in would be safe, legal, and ethical. An APA Ethics Office statement in *Psychology Today* underscored what psychologists would achieve in *all interrogations*: "The ability to spot conditions that make abuse more likely uniquely prepares psychologists for this task. Adding a trained professional ensures that *all interrogations* are conducted in a safe, legal, ethical, and effective manner that protects the individual and helps to elicit information that will prevent future acts of violence" (Hutson, 2008; italics added).

APA's claim that psychologists were uniquely qualified—in contrast to statements from other professional organizations reluctant to play a role in these interrogations—convinced military leaders.

> Pentagon officials said they would try to use only psychologists, not psychiatrists, to help interrogators devise strategies to get information from detainees at places like Guantánamo Bay, Cuba. The new policy follows by little more than two weeks an overwhelming vote by the American Psychiatric Association discouraging its members from participating in those efforts.
>
> (Lewis, 2006)

APA claimed that it was psychologists' unique qualifications for the interrogations at Abu Ghraib, Guantánamo, and Bagram that set them apart from other professionals. Other professions did not see a difference in qualifications. They saw it as a difference in ethics. In "Advocacy as Leadership," the American Psychiatric Association president wrote:

> I told the generals that psychiatrists will not participate in the interrogation of persons held in custody. Psychologists, by

contrast, had issued a position statement allowing consultations in interrogations. If you were ever wondering what makes us different from psychologists, here it is. This is a paramount challenge to our ethics. . . . Our profession is lost if we play any role in inflicting these wounds.

(Sharfstein, 2006, p. 1713)

Controversial Claims About What Psychologists Were Doing

APA's claims that psychologists' involvement ensured that all interrogations were—in a frequently repeated phrase—"safe, legal, ethical, and effective" kindled growing controversy. Newspaper reporters, congressional committees, human rights organizations, and others looked at the evidence and questioned APA's claims. They raised pointed questions about whether an array of psychologists played key roles in what the government termed "enhanced interrogations" and about whether APA, despite its policies and public statements, worked behind the scenes with the Department of Defense to make sure APA's ethics did not interfere with the interrogations at Abu Ghraib, Guantánamo, Bagram, and other sites.

The controversy grew over the years as articles from many sources discussed evidence answering those questions and challenging APA's claims. Examples include:

- "Red Cross Finds Detainee Abuse in Guantánamo" in the *New York Times* reviewed the 2003 and 2004 International Red Cross reports discussing psychologists' roles in abuses at Guantánamo (Lewis, 2004).
- "Newly Unredacted Report Confirms Psychologists Supported Illegal Interrogations in Iraq and Afghanistan" reported evidence from U.S. Department of Defense documents obtained under the Freedom of Information Act (American Civil Liberties Union, 2008).
- A U.S. Central Intelligence Agency (2004) special review of counterterrorism, detention, and interrogation activities described how an array of both outside and on-site psychologists reported no lasting harmful psychological effects from water-boarding (see also Cole, 2013; Greenberg, 2005; Greenberg & Dratel, 2005; Spetalnick, 2014).
- An open letter to APA from Amnesty International, Physicians for Human Rights, and 11 other organizations discussed APA's "providing ethical cover for psychologists' participation in

detainee abuse," "grievous mismanagement of this issue," and making a "terrible stain on the reputation of American psychology" (American Friends Service Committee, Amnesty International U.S.A., Bill of Rights Defense Committee, et al., 2009).

- The *Boston Globe* published a series of investigative reports on psychologists' involvement in enhanced interrogations and concluded with an editorial, "Psychologists and Torture," claiming: "From the moment U.S. military and civilian officials began detaining and interrogating Guantánamo Bay prisoners with methods that the Red Cross has called tantamount to torture, they have had the assistance of psychologists" (*Boston Globe*, 2008; see also Goodman, 2007).
- Eban (2007) wrote that "psychologists weren't merely complicit in America's aggressive new interrogation regime. Psychologists . . . had actually designed the tactics and trained interrogators in them. . . . "
- Mayer (2008) reported that "[General] Dunlavey soon drafted military psychologists to play direct roles in breaking detainees down. The psychologists were both treating the detainees clinically and advising interrogators on how to manipulate them and exploit their phobias . . . " (p. 196).
- Professor of Medicine and Bioethics Steven Miles, author of *Oath Betrayed: America's Torture Doctors* (Miles, 2009a) wrote: "The American Psychological Association was unique among U.S. health professional associations in providing policy cover for abusive interrogations" (Miles, 2009b).

"A Definitive, Independent, and Objective Review of . . . All Relevant Evidence" Is Commissioned

After years of new revelations and criticism, a book appeared that almost no one recognized as the turning point. *Pay Any Price*, by Pulitzer Prize–winning investigative reporter James Risen, reviewed extensive primary source documents including emails that a CIA-connected researcher had collected.

The book documented how APA's actions contrasted with its policies prohibiting torture and its public statements about working to prevent torture: "The emails reveal how the American Psychological Association (APA), the nation's largest professional group for psychologists, put its seal of approval on those close ties [among leading psychologists and CIA and Pentagon officials] and thus indirectly on torture" (Risen, 2014, p. 178).

Pay Any Price used the CIA-connected researcher's collection of emails along with other primary source documents to expose how APA's public statements about ethics and torture were not just empty but misleading: "America's psychologists, who also knew the truth, also remained silent.... Worse, they participated, and quietly changed their profession's ethics code to allow torture to continue. In return, the psychologists were showered with government money and benefits" (Risen, 2014, p. 177).

A common tendency of many organizations and individuals when criticized is to deny and discredit the criticisms. At first APA denied Risen's claims and tried to discredit his book, as it had tried to deny and discredit prior investigative reports. The organization attacked Risen's methods and conclusions. The prestige and influence that APA had gained during a history stretching back well over a century, along with the sheer size and diversity of the membership backing its claims, gave the organization great credibility and authority.

APA (2014a) issued a press release describing the book's claims as "absurd," "inaccurate," "one-sided reporting," "mischaracterization," and "innuendo," while asserting that APA fosters "the highest ethical standards." APA again stressed its "longstanding position against torture," its "no-exceptions prohibition against the use of specific abusive techniques," its new "Reaffirmation of the APA Position Against Torture," and its policy "that prohibits psychologists from working in unlawful national security detention settings unless they are working directly for the detainee or for a third party to protect human rights or they are providing treatment to military personnel." APA stated that it communicated this policy "to the president, the attorney general, heads of CIA and the Defense Department, and the chairs and ranking members of all congressional committees with jurisdiction."

Despite APA's vigorous refutation, *Pay Any Price* brought the controversy to the tipping point. The carefully documented evidence Risen had published in his book made it difficult to deny and disparage.

APA then took a surprising step that involved immense courage, leadership, and risk. In a remarkable move toward transparency, APA decided to authorize an investigation by a former federal prosecutor who would use his independent judgment—rather than be directed and restrained by the organization—in pursuing the evidence and facts wherever they might lead.

The move acknowledged the obvious: That APA—like *any* organization—was unlikely to be free of significant bias and inherent conflicts of interest when weighing and responding to charges of improper behavior. (Human nature suggests that were corporations, small businesses, and other organizations allowed to render the final verdict when charged with breaking the law, the outcomes might be significantly different than when judged by a judge or jury.)

APA (2014b) announced this new approach in a second press release that began:

> The American Psychological Association (APA) Board of Directors has reviewed the allegation in James Risen's book, Pay Any Price: Greed, Power and Endless War, that APA colluded with the Bush administration to support torture during the war on terror. Specifically, Risen alleges that APA supported the development and implementation of "enhanced" interrogation techniques that constituted torture, and was complicit with the CIA and U.S. military to this end. We believe that APA's October 16th statement refuting Risen's assertion was a fair and accurate response. However, the allegation made by Mr. Risen is highly charged and very serious. His book has created confusion for the public and APA members. This confusion, coupled with the seriousness of the allegation, requires a definitive, independent and objective review of the allegation and all relevant evidence. Toward that end, and to fulfill its values of transparency and integrity, the APA Board has authorized the engagement of David Hoffman of the law firm Sidley Austin to conduct an independent review of whether there is any factual support for the assertion that APA engaged in activity that would constitute collusion with the Bush administration to promote, support or facilitate the use of "enhanced" interrogation techniques by the United States in the war on terror.
>
> (APA, 2014b)

This Independent Review Report, commonly known as the Hoffman report (Hoffman et al., 2015a, 2015b), uncovered additional emails and other documents that both supported and extended the reporting in Risen's book. It also validated works by investigative reporters, human rights organizations, and others who examined evidence contrasting APA's public policies and statements in the area of ethics with its behavior behind the scenes.

Reporting from APA's annual convention the following month, the *Chronicle of Higher Education* summarized the report's immediate aftermath (see also Ackerman, 2015):

> The association has faced withering scrutiny since the publication of a report that found that it had colluded with the military

to establish loose ethics guidelines regarding interrogations of terrorism suspects. . . . Essentially, the report says, the group turned a blind eye to psychologists involved in what many now call torture. The report . . . also detailed a dysfunctional culture among the group's leadership . . . with examples of bullying of critics.

(Wilhelm, 2015)

The report's revelations drew comment from other organizations. The Canadian Psychological Association (CPA, 2015) issued a bulletin emphasizing human rights, international humanitarian law, and accountability (see also statements from the European Federation of Psychologists' Associations, 2015; British Psychological Society, 2015):

> The Canadian Psychological Association (CPA) was saddened to learn of the findings of the Hoffman report. . . . The CPA holds itself and the discipline and profession of psychology to standards of international humanitarian law. . . . It is CPA's opinion and practice that the discipline and profession of psychology hold itself accountable in all matters of policy, education, research, and practice regarding human rights and the health and welfare of individuals and societies.

The Association for Psychological Science (APS) Executive Director said: "The American Psychological Association has abused its privileged position and failed miserably in its responsibility to protect the public" (quoted by Marklein, 2015).

The Executive Director of Physicians for Human Rights wrote that APA "must take stock of the pain and suffering it caused by contributing to the torture program. It must . . . recognise the corruption that fueled an unconscionable dismantling of ethical standards aimed at ensuring that psychologists do no harm" (McKay, 2015).

Learning From the Past and Research Studies to Face the Future

With that context in mind, we can see how this case study—combined with research findings and other examples—suggests 5 practical steps to strengthen ethics in organizations and individuals. Each of the 5 brief chapters that follow highlights one of those steps.

References

Ackerman, S. (2015, July 10). U.S. torture doctors could face charges after report alleges post-9/11 "collusion"; Leading group of psychologists faces a reckoning following repeated denials that its members were complicit in Bush administration-era torture. *The Guardian*. Retrieved from www.theguardian.com/law/2015/jul/10/us-torture-doctors-psycholo gists-apa-prosecution

Aldhaus, P. (2015, August 5). Psychology is in crisis over role in Bush-era torture: At a huge meeting in Toronto, psychologists are grappling with their role in the U.S. government's use of torture; "We've got a fire in our house, and it's a devastating fire," one psychologist told BuzzFeed News. *BuzzFeed News*. Retrieved from www.buzzfeed.com/peteraldhous/ psychologists-grapple-with-torture

American Civil Liberties Union. (2008, April). *Newly unredacted report confirms psychologists supported illegal interrogations in Iraq and Afghanistan* [Press release]. Retrieved from http://bit.ly/97hxR4

American Friends Service Committee, Pacific Southwest Region, Amnesty International USA, Bill of Rights Defense Committee, Center for Constitutional Rights, Coalition for an Ethical Psychology, . . . Psychologists for Social Responsibility. (2009). *Open letter in response to the American Psychological Association Board*. Retrieved from http://ethicalpsycho logy.org/materials/Letter-APA-Board-6-29-09.pdf

American Psychological Association. (2007a). *Reaffirmation of the American Psychological Association position against torture and other cruel, inhuman, or degrading treatment or punishment and its application to individuals defined in the United States code as "enemy combatants."* Retrieved from www.apa.org/about/policy/torture.aspx

American Psychological Association. (2007b). *Statement of the American Psychological Association on psychology and interrogations submitted to the United States Senate Select Committee on Intelligence*. Retrieved from www.apa.org/ethics/programs/position/legislative/senate-select.aspx

American Psychological Association. (2014a). *APA response to Risen book and allegations of support for torture* [Press release]. Retrieved from www.apa.org/news/press/response/risen-book.aspx

American Psychological Association. (2014b). *Statement of APA Board of Directors: Outside counsel to conduct independent review of allegations of support for torture* [Press release]. Retrieved from www.apa.org/news/ press/releases/2014/11/risenallegations.aspx

Boston Globe. (2008, August). Boston Globe editorial: Psychologists and torture. *Boston Globe*. Retrieved from http://bit.ly/c1t0mK

Canadian Psychological Association. (2015). *CPA response to the American Psychological Association's Hoffman review [Bulletin]*. Retrieved from www.cpa.ca/bulletins

Cole, D. (2013). *Torture memos: Rationalizing the unthinkable*. New York, NY: The New Press.

Eban, K. (2007, July 17). Rorschach and awe. *Vanity Fair*. Retrieved from http://bit.ly/aAbkCu

Goodman, A. (2007, June 8). Psychologists implicated in torture. *Seattle Post-Intelligencer*. Retrieved from www.seattlepi.com/opinion/318745_amy07.html

Greenberg, K. J. (Ed.). (2005). *The torture debate in America*. New York, NY: Cambridge University Press.

Greenberg, K. J., & Dratel, J. L. (Eds.) (2005). *The torture papers: The road to Abu Ghraib*. New York, NY: Cambridge University Press.

Hoffman, D. H., Carter, D. J., Lopez, C. R. V., Benzmiller, H. L., Guo, A. X., Latifi, S. Y., & Craig, D. C. (2015a). *Report to the Special Committee of the Board of Directors of the American Psychological Association: Independent review relating to APA ethics guidelines, national security interrogations, and torture*. Chicago, IL: Sidley Austin LLP. Retrieved from www.apa.org/independent-review/APA-FINAL-Report-7.2.15.pdf

Hoffman, D. H., Carter, D. J., Lopez, C. R. V., Benzmiller, H. L., Guo, A. X., Latifi, S. Y., & Craig, D. C. (2015b). *Report to the Special Committee of the Board of Directors of the American Psychological Association: Independent review relating to APA ethics guidelines, national security interrogations, and torture (revised)*. Chicago, IL: Sidley Austin LLP. Retrieved from www.apa.org/independent-review/revised-report.pdf

Hutson, M. (2008). Keeping interrogation clean. *Psychology Today*. Retrieved from https://www.psychologytoday.com/articles/200611/keeping-interrogation-clean

Lewis, N. A. (2004, November). Red Cross finds detainee abuse in Guantanamo. *New York Times*. Retrieved from www.nytimes.com/2004/11/30/politics/red-cross-finds-detainee-abuse-in-guantanamo.html

Lewis, N. A. (2006, June). Military alters the makeup of interrogation advisers. *New York Times*. Retrieved from http://nyti.ms/9aRWIq

Marklein, M. B. (2015, July). Psychologists in crisis over findings on 'torture' allegations. *University World News*. Retrieved from www.universityworldnews.com/article.php?story=20150717125853305

Mayer, J. (2008). *The dark side*. New York, NY: Doubleday.

McDaniel, S., & Kaslow, N. (2015a, August 14). *Email message sent by APA President-elect Susan H. McDaniel, PhD, and Past President Nadine J. Kaslow, PhD, ABPP, to all APA members*. Retrieved from www.apa.org/independent-review/member-letter.aspx

McDaniel, S., & Kaslow, N. (2015b, July 24). *Letter to APA members from APA President-Elect Susan McDaniel, PhD, and APA Past President Nadine J. Kaslow, PhD, ABPP, members of the Special Committee for the Independent Review*. Washington, DC: American Psychological Association. Retrieved from www.apa.org/independent-review/letter-members-apology.pdf

McDaniel, S., & Kaslow, N. (2015c, July 21). *Letter to psychology colleagues in the international community from APA President-Elect Susan McDaniel, PhD, and APA Past President Nadine J. Kaslow, PhD, ABPP, members of the Special Committee for the Independent Review*. Washington, DC: American Psychological Association. Retrieved from www.apa.org/independent-review/international-letter.pdf

McKay, M. (2015, August). The brutal toll of psychologists' role in torture. *Huffington Post*. Retrieved from www.huffingtonpost.com/donna-mckay/the-brutal-toll-of-psycho_b_7948448.html

Miles, S. H. (2009a). *Oath betrayed* (2nd ed.). Los Angeles, CA, USA: University of California Press.

Miles, S. H. (2009b, May). Psychologists and torture [Letter to the editor published online]. *British Medical Journal*. Retrieved from www.bmj.com/rapid-response/2011/11/02/psychologists-and-torture

Risen, J. (2014). *Pay any price: Greed, power, and endless war*. New York, NY: Houghton Mifflin Harcourt.

Sharfstein, S. (2006). Presidential address: Advocacy as leadership. *American Journal of Psychiatry*, *163*, 1711–1715. Retrieved from http://dx.doi.org/10.1176/ajp.2006.163.10.1711

Spetalnick, M. (2014). Psychologist admits he waterboarded al Qaeda suspects. *Reuters*. Retrieved from http://www.reuters.com/article/us-usa-cia-torture-psychologist-idUSKBN0JT2DB20141215.

U.S. Central Intelligence Agency, Inspector General. (2004). *Special review: Counterterrorrism detention and interrogation activities, Appendix C.* Langley, VA: Central Intelligence Agency.

Wilhelm, I. (2015). Meeting of psychologists becomes a moment of soul searching. *Chronicle of Higher Education*. Retrieved from http://chronicle.com/article/A-Meeting-of-Psychologists/232267

3 Making Codes Work

Why do so many good ethics codes do so little good?

Some wonderful codes find a welcoming home in public relations and contract a severe care of agoraphobia, never setting foot outside home. The organization points with pride to its stellar ethics code that highlights high ideals and admirable aspirations while banning questionable conduct. The code holds a halo of presumed good behavior over the organization while giving a warm sense of reassurance to the board of directors, auditors, inspectors, site visitors, investors, and the public. It does little else.

Even ethics codes backed by good-faith enforcement can fall short of fostering an ethically strong organization. Unethical acts may go unnoticed, noticed acts may go unreported, reported acts may not be fully and fairly investigated, and findings from investigations may gather dust instead of guiding responses to ethical problems.

We can take a good first step toward strengthening ethics in an organization and the people within the organization if we can make sure its ethics code works. An organization can have an exceptional ethics code,[1] but who cares? A good place to begin this step is to ask not only who cares about the code, but why. Of course, if there is no written statement of encouraged, expected, or required standards of behavior, that alone suggests a potentially useful intervention.

Codes in Context

Codes can help us strengthen ethics in organizations and individuals only if they are rooted in a context of caring in the organization and in the individuals who make up that organization. The caring context is reflected in leaders who model ethical behavior and address ethical issues; in training that focuses on the ethics code, its values, and its practical implications; in a person (e.g., ombudsperson), committee, or office that responds effectively to ethics questions and complaints; in people throughout the organization accepting, respecting, and embracing the code as *their* own code; in the presence of ethics in the day-to-day planning, decision-making, and questioning as people carry out the work of the organization; and in the way the code and its values are woven into the other aims of the organization (e.g., to make or sell products; provide services; raise awareness and support causes or candidates).

The lack of a strong context of caring about ethics can show itself in many ways. Do people in some departments or levels of the organization view the code as a burden—needlessly getting in the way of their work as they believe it should be done—pressed down on them from above by those in power who don't understand the jobs they do and the best way to do them? Or is the ethics code an empty formality, not to be taken seriously? Or as a guide for documenting that things were done the "right" way, the resulting documentation having no relation whatsoever to how things were actually done?

A widely admired and copied code illustrates the illusions that codes out of context can create. *Fortune*'s annual survey of around 10,000 executives, directors, and securities analysts named Enron the "most innovative company" six years in a row. It was the 18th most admired company and among the top 5 in quality of management (Enron, 2001). In addition to its creativity and its financial success, Enron touted another accomplishment: its famous ethics code.

Enron had created a thoughtful, comprehensive, practical code that could guide the behavior of everyone who worked for the organization. Every employee was required to read and sign the 84-page code, which was widely praised for years as a model for other groups (some of whom adopted it) wishing to achieve Enron's reputation for integrity, innovation, and profitability.

A few years later, Enron's code of ethics shifted from fame to notoriety as prosecutors used it to cross-examine employees in trials that convicted 21 felons after the company collapsed into what at the time was the largest bankruptcy in United States history and caused investors to lose $74 billion, with losses due to fraud up to $45 billion (Arbogast, 2013; Axtman, 2005; McLean & Elkind, 2013; Merle, 2016; Pasha, 2006; Watkins, 2013).

Decades of research support the view that an ethics code not firmly rooted in organizational context and culture tends to be an empty gesture, failing to strengthen ethics within the organization and among individuals who make up the organization. In the early 1990s, for example, Rebecca Goodell (1994, 1996), working with the Ethics Resource Center (ERC) and the market research firm NFO, surveyed thousands of people in corporations about the ethics of their organizations in the ECR's first National Business Survey. The results suggested that when a code was ingrained in the culture of the organization (as reflected in ethics training, an ethics office that heard complaints about violations and gave advice to those with questions, and so on), it tended to encourage ethical behavior. However, the existence of a code that was not ingrained in the organizational culture was linked to views that organizational behavior was less ethical. Strikingly, organizations with ethics codes that were *not* rooted in the organizational culture were viewed as behaving *less* ethically than organizations with no ethics code at all.

Lease (2006) wrote that "the literature supports . . . the contention that an ethical organizational culture cannot be created through the imposition of a code" (p. 29) but that a code can play a key role if those at the top provide ethical leadership by modeling ethical behavior and creating a culture of commitment to ethics throughout the organization (see also Bachmann, 2017; Sauser & Sims, 2015).

Kish-Gephart, Harrison, and Treviño's (2010) meta-analysis found that the "mere existence of a code of conduct has no detectable impact on unethical choices, despite the considerable amount of statistical power that comes from doing a meta-analytic summary" (p. 21). However, the study also found "a strong, negative link . . . between code enforcement and unethical choice" (p. 13; see also Singh, 2011).

Weaver (2014) noted that "empirical research has been clear" that organizational codes *per se* have "limited, if any, influence on ethical behavior" (p. 293) but must be part of an organization climate in which ethical issues are discussed on an everyday basis and become an ordinary aspect of decision-making and behavior (see also Nicholson, 2008; Weiss, 2014). The organization's ethical culture becomes internalized as part of each individual's personal values (Hill, Jones, & Schilling, 2014).

High ethical standards interwoven with the organization's other aims tend to be more effective not only in encouraging ethical behavior but also in benefiting the organization's other aims. The STR Team (a research company focusing on global data benchmarking, analytics, and marketplace dynamics) concluded that "both research as well as corporate practice from around the world has demonstrated . . . that being ethical and socially responsible actually enhances share prices and profitability in the longer term" (STR Team, 2015). Jiang, Hu, Hong, Liao, and Liu (2016) noted that "service excellence has become a strategic imperative for service organizations" and that their research findings pointed to a second "indispensable and complementary route to service success: in addition to emphasizing service excellence, organizations should highlight high ethical standards to uniquely inhibit unethical behavior. Additionally, both excellent service behavior and adherence to ethics functioned synergistically" (p. 1553; see also Jackson & Nelson, 2004).

Similarly, McMurrian and Matulich (2016) noted that "high standards of organizational ethics can contribute to profitability by reducing the cost of business transactions, building a foundation of trust with stakeholders, contributing to an internal environment of successful teamwork, and maintaining social capital that is part of an organization's market-place image" (p. 83; see also Perry, 2015). Donaldson (2000) reviewed research showing that when ethical standards were *not* interwoven, they could foster unethical behavior that would not be obvious to the public: " 'decoupled' ethical policies appear to conform to external expectations while making it easy to insulate much of the organization from those expectations."

These and other studies suggest that codes are most likely to prompt ethical thinking and action when rooted in an ecology of strong ethical leadership, effective enforcement, a culture of ethical concern, and the other aims of the organization. Ethics questions can rise for everyone to the level of daily concern often devoted to questions of profits, promotions, and will this meeting ever end?

How One Organization Created a Model Code

The American Psychological Association (APA) pioneered a fascinating approach to creating a code. The organization had grown for over half a century without an ethics code. Early reports attributed APA's founding to a landmark July 8, 1892, organizational meeting at Clark University. The participants included Stanley Hall, George Fullerton, Joseph Jastrow, William James, George Ladd, James Cattell, and Mark Baldwin at Clark University (Fernberger, 1943). Interestingly, a psychologist working on a history of the organization tried to gather and verify information about this meeting. He discovered that two of psychologists who allegedly attended the meeting (Cattell and Jastrow) denied attending, and failed to find *any* supportive evidence that the historic meeting ever happened. He reached a conclusion worth considering when examining minutes or other documents of an organization: "All of this leads to a possible conclusion—and I say this as an ex-Secretary of the Association—that one cannot always trust the printed minutes . . . as evidence of what actually happened at any meeting" (Fernberger, 1943, p. 35). Fernberger's healthy skepticism about minutes as an accurate reflection of what happened at a meeting is a useful reminder of the importance of going beyond minutes, mission statements, public relations documents, and other written records. Talking with people at all levels of the organization and searching for other kinds of information can be invaluable when taking steps to strengthen organizational ethics.

Whatever its beginnings, APA grew in size and scope, and as it grew, the ethics problems encountered by its members grew in diversity and complexity. In 1939, APA charged its Committee on Scientific and Professional Ethics (CSPE) with figuring out whether a written ethics code was needed. Eight years later, the Committee recommended that APA develop a written code because "unwritten code is tenuous, elusive, and unsatisfactory" ("A little recent history," 1952, p. 426). Edward Tolman chaired a new Committee on Ethical Standards, which would map out an approach to creating the code.

The final decision on whether to have a written code was argued throughout the organization, at meetings, and in the pages of APA's journal of record, *American Psychologist*. Calvin Hall was among the prominent and influential psychologists arguing against a code. In an article, "Crooks, Codes, and Cant" in *American Psychologist*, Hall argued that ethical psychologists did not need a code and that crooked psychologists would study the code to discover what they could get away with. He wrote: "I am convinced that laws are made for the benefit of the lawless and not for the lawful and that the 'Psychologists' Code' if it is adopted will give aid to our errant brothers by suggesting opportunities for shady practices" (p. 430). The subsequent code, then, grew out of, benefitted from, and was shaped by this deliberative process in which all voices and views were heard and considered.

APA adopted an unprecedented approach to creating a code. The new method departed sharply from the customary approach used by over 500 other professional and business organizations (Hobbs, 1948). APA viewed psychology as an empirical discipline and wanted to use the tools of its own discipline to create a code. The empirical approach to creating a code differed from the traditional method, which Hobbs called the "armchair approach" (p. 82) in which a special committee, presumably made up of those most qualified, would study the codes of other organizations, review the literature on ethics, and discuss the issues, and issue calls for suggestions in publications or other documents (but not contact each individual member specifically for this purpose, as opposed to bundling the call with other matters).

APA's radically new approach was based on psychological science, specifically on survey research. APA would actively reach out to its members individually, sending each a letter asking about that member's personal experiences. These individual letters could create a direct connection between each member and the committee that might go missing were the call published in journals, bundled among other matters, or made in more general announcements that members might or might not happen to notice. The method underscored that the committee wanted the code to grow out of the views of all members and not just those in the inner circles or those more actively involved in the organization. It gave all members a stake in the code and a role in shaping it. Members would know that their own experiences and views were part of the code's foundation.

The use of this method helped create the crucial context of caring about the code. It rooted the code firmly in APA's organizational context and culture, a product of psychology's empirical tools. Hobbs wrote that this method created "a code of ethics truly indigenous to psychology, a code that could be lived" (Hobbs, 1948, p. 84). Sanford wrote in the "Summary Report of the 1952 Meeting" that "Many will agree that this action represents the most significant single step in the history of psychology as a profession" (p. 636).

Drift

All revisions of the code were to use the same method of reaching out to each member individually to ask for "additional critical incidents of controversial behavior" (Holtzman, 1960, p. 247). Sending a survey form to every member individually would preserve, renew, and reinforce the stake that all members had in the ethics code, would sustain this unique empirical approach indigenous to psychology that created "a code that could be lived," would reflect the experiences and values of the full range of membership, and would foster loyalty to the code as the product of fully shared authorship among the members.

Putting the same methodology to use in revising the code as in creating the original code also drew on psychological understandings of group process, management style, empowerment, and allegiance (e.g., Golann, 1969; Hobbs, 1948; Holtzman, 1960). Reaching out individually to all members for the primary data of revision was considered to produce a very different code than other methods of updating a code. It would empower all members through meaningful individual involvement at the ground level of the revision process, benefit from better organizational dynamics by fostering a psychological sense of community among those who made up the organization, and create a better revision. Maintaining this methodology to revise the code preserved an empirically based code "based upon the day-to-day decisions made by psychologists in the practice of their profession, rather than prescribed by a committee" (Golann, 1969, p. 454). Surveying all members individually created a revision "close enough to the contemporary scene to win the genuine acceptance of the majority who are most directly affected by its principles" (Holtzman, 1960, p. 250).

Unfortunately, there was a drift away from this remarkable method for revising the code. That drift and other changes laid the groundwork for some of the unfortunate outcomes discussed in this book.

Assessment for Action

When thinking through possible approaches to strengthening ethics in a specific organization, it may be useful to consider some of the following questions.

- What person, committee, or department was responsible for creating or revising the organization's ethics code?
- Who (individuals, groups, committees, and departments) was consulted in creating or revising the code?
- Who was *not* consulted in creating or revising the code?
- How long has the current code been in existence? Are parts of it in need of revision?
- Does everyone in the organization have a copy of the code? If not, why not?
- How do the people who make up the organization learn about the code and its implications for their role in the organization?
- What officer, office, or committee, if any, is responsible for responding to questions about ethical issues or dilemmas? Do people at all levels of the organization view this officer, office, or committee as knowledgeable, trustworthy, fair, and helpful?
- What officer, office, or committee, if any, is responsible for hearing and responding to ethics complaints? Do people at all levels of the organization view this officer, office, or committee as knowledgeable, trustworthy, fair, and helpful?
- To what degree, if any, is the code enforced? How is it enforced?
- To what degree are leaders seen as valuing, supporting, and living up to the ethics code?

- To what degree do people in the organization view it as *their own* code (rather than an externally imposed decree), expressing their values?
- To what degree do people respect and value the code, seeing it as important and helpful?

In some situations, it may be helpful to survey those who make up the organization along with other stakeholders about these issues, asking them about needed changes. The results may provide an opportunity to open up discussions. Depending on the organization, assuring that the survey is anonymous may gather responses that are more frank, comprehensive, and useful.

Note

1 What serves the function of an ethics code goes by different names in different organizations. It may be called the code of conduct, the statement of values, standards and practices, and so on. For the sake of economy and convenience, "ethics code" will be a stand-in for all those different terms.

References

Arbogast, S. V. (2013). *Resisting corporate corruption: Cases in practical ethics from Enron through the financial crisis*. New York, NY: Wiley.

Axtman, K. (2005, June 20). How Enron awards do, or don't, trickle down. *Christian Science Monitor*. Retrieved from www.csmonitor.com/2005/0620/p02s01-usju.html

Bachmann, B. (2017). *Ethical leadership in organizations* [Kindle for the Mac version]. New York, NY: Springer.

Donaldson, T. (2000, November 13). Adding corporate ethics to the bottom line. *Financial Times*. Retrieved from http://bit.ly/2kiqxZi

Enron Corporation. (2001, February 6). *Enron named most innovative for sixth year*. Retrieved from www.prnewswire.com/news-releases/enron-named-most-innovative-for-sixth-year-71240567.html

Fernberger, S. W. (1943). American psychological association: 1892–1942. *Psychological Review, 50*(1), 33–60.

Golann, S. E. (1969). Emerging areas of ethical concern. *American Psychologist, 24*(4), 454–459.

Goodell, R. (1994). *Ethics in American business: Policies, programs and perceptions: Report of a landmark survey of US employees*. Washington, DC: Ethics Resource Center.

Goodell, R. (1996). The Ethics Resource Center's survey of ethics practices and employee perceptions. In R. P. Conaboy (Ed.), *Corporate crime in*

America: Strengthening the "good citizen" corporation: Proceedings of the Second Symposium on Crime and Punishment in the United States, September 7–8, 1995 (pp. 159–173). Washington, DC: United States Sentencing Commission.

Hall, C. (1952). Crooks, codes, and cant. *American Psychologist, 7*(8), 430–431.

Hill, C. W., Jones, G. R., & Schilling, M. A. (2014). *Strategic management: Theory and cases: An integrated approach* (11th ed.). Boston, MA: Cengage.

Hobbs, N. (1948). The development of a code of ethical standards for psychology. *American Psychologist, 3*(3), 80–84.

Holtzman, W. H. (1960). Some problems of defining ethical behavior. *American Psychologist, 15*(4), 247–250.

Jackson, I. A., & Nelson, J. (2004). *Profits with principles: Seven strategies for delivering value with values.* New York City: Broadway Business.

Jiang, K., Hu, J., Hong, Y., Liao, H., & Liu, S. (2016). Do it well and do it right: The impact of service climate and ethical climate on business performance and the boundary conditions. *Journal of Applied Psychology, 101*(11), 1553–1568.

Kish-Gephart, J. J., Harrison, D. A., & Treviño, L. K. (2010). Bad apples, bad cases, and bad barrels: Meta-analytic evidence about sources of unethical decisions at work. *Journal of Applied Psychology, 95*(1), 1–31.

Lease, D. R. (2006). *From great to ghastly: How toxic organizational cultures poison companies: The rise and fall of Enron, WorldCom, HealthSouth, and Tyco International.* Retrieved from www.scribd.com/doc/74367362/DavidLease-Great-to-Ghastly

A little recent history. (1952). *American Psychologist, 7*(8), 426–428.

McLean, B., & Elkind, P. (2013). *The smartest guys in the room: The amazing rise and scandalous fall of Enron.* New York, NY: Penguin.

McMurrian, R. C., & Matulich, E. (2016). Building customer value and profitability with business ethics. *Journal of Business & Economics Research, 14*(3), 83–90.Merle, R. (2016, December 9). Criminal business executives just don't get why they're in jail. *Washington Post.* Retrieved from http://wapo.st/2kxEEbO

Nicholson, L. H. (2008). Culture is the key to employee adherence to corporate codes of ethics. *Journal of Business & Technology Law, 3*, 449–454.

Pasha, S. (2006, April 26). Lay, prosecutor clash at trial. *CNN.* Retrieved from http://money.cnn.com/2006/04/26/news/newsmakers/enron_trial/

Perry, E. (2015, October 11). Good corporate governance can improve a company's bottom line. *Telegraph.* Retrieved from http://bit.ly/2jEvcCV

Sanford, F. H. (1952). Summary report on the 1952 annual meeting. *American Psychologist, 7*(11), 634–644.

Sauser, W. I. Jr., & Sims, R. R. (2015). Techniques for preparing business students to contribute to ethical organizational cultures. In *Handbook of research on business ethics and corporate responsibilities* (pp. 221–248). Hersey, PA: IGI Global.

Singh, J. B. (2011). Determinants of the effectiveness of corporate codes of ethics: An empirical study. *Journal of Business Ethics, 101*(3), 385–395.

STR Team. (2015, December 21). Being good is good for business: Research demonstrates that being ethical and socially responsible contribute to higher profitability. *Business Standard.* Retrieved from www.business-standard.com/article/management/being-good-is-good-for-business-115122000612_1.html

Watkins, S. S. (2013). Foreword. In S. V. Arbogast (Ed.), *Resisting corporate corruption: Cases in practical ethics from Enron through the financial crisis* (pp. ix–xii). New York, NY: Wiley.

Weaver, G. R. (2014). Encouraging ethics in organizations: A review of some key research findings. *American Criminal Law Review, 51,* 293–317.

Weiss, J. W. (2014). *Business ethics: A stakeholder and issues management approach* (6th ed.). San Francisco, CA: Berrett-Koehler.

4 "Your Call Is Very Important to Us"
Finding and Closing Gaps

All organizations that lack perfection (i.e., all organizations) have gaps. Gaps can run between the organization as it actually is and the face it paints out front for the public, between what it says and what it does, between expense reports and the amount spent (and how it was spent), between the income reported on tax forms and the money actually taken in, between the minutes of a meeting and what in fact happened at the meeting, between the documented reasons for promotions and firings and the real reasons, between heavily promoted policies of transparency and what is kept hidden, between representing products or services as safe and the actual risks, and on and on and on. A second step, then, to strengthen ethics in an organization and the individuals who make up the organization is to look for the gaps so that they can be closed. This simple-sounding step is actually, as Downe, Cowell, and Morgan (2016) point out, more of a struggle against competing values, frameworks, and incentives: "The enhancement of conduct across an organization can be seen . . . as a struggle to assert the importance of a particular set of principles in the face of other bases for judgment."

As members of an organization, we can remain blissfully unaware of gaps either by failing to notice them or by keeping our eyes shut tight against what we don't want to know. But often members know where the gaps are. For example, in *Study on Military Professionalism*, Ulmer wrote:

> Officers of all grades perceive a significant difference between the ideal values and the actual or operative values of the Officer Corps. This perception is strong, clear, pervasive, and statistically and qualitatively independent of grade, branch, educational level, or source of commission . . .
>
> (Ulmer, 1970, iii)

The Wells Fargo Bank scandal provides a vivid example of employees' awareness of the stark chasm between the rules that management kept repeating and a more powerful competing incentive (Cowley, 2016a, 2016b; Corkery & Cowley, 2016; Glazer, 2016; Zoltners, Sinha, & Lorimer, 2016). Wells Fargo laid down strict rules against opening sham bank accounts or credit cards without the knowledge or approval of the customer. It held ethics workshops to emphasize the rules. It sent out risk professionals to make sure employees heard this message loud and clear. And yet . . . It also imposed a competing incentive—sales goals that were virtually impossible to meet without cheating—that carried more force. As one former Wells Fargo banker put it: "They warned us about this type of behavior and said, 'You must report it,' but the reality was that people had to meet their goals . . . They needed a paycheck" (Corkery & Cowley, 2016).

Gaps represent a betrayal of honesty and trust. We are invited to trust that what is said or written about the organizations and the people in the organization is true, but our trust is betrayed. Some betrayals may seem relatively minor and may occur to us as we sit for long periods of time on hold listening to a recording assuring us of how very important our phone call is. It doesn't seem to be important enough to avoid wasting our time making us sit on hold or to hire enough staff to answer phone calls promptly, but it gives us time to consider how they might treat us if our call were *not* all that important.

The empty ritual of assuring us that something is very important has become routine once an organization has made a huge blunder or becomes involved in scandal or other bad publicity. Once the matter becomes public, someone in the organization rushes forward to assure us that its great priority has *always* been devoting exceptional time, resources, skill, and care to make sure such blunders or scandals never occur. Here are 10 examples:

- When a hospital mixed up two charts, resulting in one woman getting a mastectomy she did not need and a delay in another woman's cancer treatment, a hospital spokesperson assured the public that "the hospital does everything it can to ensure patient safety" ("Patient gets needless mastectomy after hospital mix-up; Halifax-area hospital authority apologizes as 2 separate mistakes revealed," 2013). Apparently, doing "everything" does not include making sure you're operating on the right patient or that you've got the right patient's chart.
- When it was reported one Veterans Administration whistle-blower, a clinical psychologist, had been falsely discredited as

a drug dealer, another whistleblower had been discounted as a bad employee, and fewer than 10% of the complaints were even investigated, the Deputy Inspector emphasized that "I made it a high priority and my first priority to reinforce that the OIG [Office of Inspector General] values whistleblowers" (Slack, 2015).

- When an investigation of a prominent university center found that for almost a decade the female faculty endured not only "a climate of conflict, tension, hostility and mistrust" but also "unprofessional, demeaning" treatment, a spokesperson for the school of medicine assured everyone that, contrary to the information uncovered by the investigation, actually the "leadership within the university and the health system is committed to a work environment that is welcoming and free from discrimination of any kind" (Gordon, 2015).
- When a regional trustee in one of the Canadian provinces used a racial slur (the "N" word) to refer to one of the parents in a public meeting, the Education Minister was quick to assure everyone that it was a "priority" that "racism and discrimination are not tolerated in our educational system" (Javed & Rushowy, 2017).
- When it was reported that "previously unreleased reports by the Army, Navy and Air Force reveal numerous cases where military officials knew or suspected that child abuse or neglect was occurring—but failed to intervene or to alert the Family Advocacy Program or state child welfare agencies," a Pentagon spokesperson explained that despite these numerous cases where officials decided against intervening, "The welfare of our service members and their family members warrants the highest priority in the Department of Defense. . . . The department is actively committed to keeping children safe and healthy" (Cloud, 2016).
- When the National Health Service of England was fined £1,300,000 for careless treatment of sensitive information such as "lost laptops, files left at a grocery shop and records abandoned at a bus stop," an NHS spokesperson was quick to offer assurance that despite the impression given by all these instances, "protecting the security of data across government and especially within the health system is a top priority" Scannell & Chon, 2015).
- When a university paid $3,300,000 in fines and restitution for deceptive marketing practices, a spokesperson for the university claimed that "student achievement is our top priority" (Cotton, 2013).
- When it was reported that not only had information on veterans who had died been mailed to other veterans' surviving spouses

but also staff had snooped into the files of veterans who had killed themselves, a Veterans Administration official emphasized that despite these reports, patient privacy was a "top priority": "Inappropriate access of patient health records, either during or post treatment, is absolutely unacceptable" (Waldman & Ornstein, 2015).

- When a McDonald chicken nuggets supplier was shown on video engaging in animal cruelty ("workers were seen stabbing, beating and stomping on chickens in an undercover video shot by animal rights activists"), the company that contracted this supplier issued a written statement that "Animal well-being is a priority at our company . . ." ("McDonald's drops nuggets supplier after video shows animal cruelty," 2015).

- When the school psychologist was sentenced to prison for pornographic videos of children, the school district—which had screened and hired this person as the *best* candidate among all applicants to work with children—issued a statement that the "County School District's top priority is the safety and well-being of its students. . . . " (Roustan, 2015; see also Mojica, 2015).

Gaps between what organizations say and reality may have become so common, routine, and clichéd that we no longer notice them. They hide in plain sight, part of the familiar background that we no longer pay any attention to. But these gaps, as noted earlier, represent a betrayal of honesty and trust, and their numbing repetition and familiarity mask their true costs. In their book *Trust and Betrayal in the Workplace*, Reina and Reina (2015) note research suggesting that 90% of employees frequently experience relatively minor betrayals of trust at work, but ignore them or sweep them aside. The costs of these gaps and the betrayals they represent range from seemingly minor wrongs to people dying, as in the GM example described in Chapter 1. GM betrayed its customers, who trusted and relied on the company's honesty, integrity, and good faith. There was a gap between what GM was telling its customers about the safety of its cars and what it knew about the design flaw and how it could cause harm or death to GM drivers and passengers. As a result, some GM customers died. Others suffered needless catastrophic injuries. Families suddenly lost a mother, a father, a child, or another loved one. These are some of the true costs of deciding that fixing a design flaw is "not worth the cost" (Viscusi, 2015, p. 7).

Research supports the idea that betrayal *per se* can cause harm and may deepen the response to other bad acts. Rachman (2010) noted that betrayal's effects may include "shock, loss and grief, morbid pre-occupation, damaged self-esteem, self-doubting, anger" and sometimes "life-altering changes" (p. 304). Koehler and Gershoff's (2003) studies "found that people reacted more strongly . . . to acts of betrayal than to identical bad acts that do not violate a duty or promise to protect" (p. 244; see also Beamish, 2001).

Research also supports the idea that when betrayal happens within organizational dynamics, it may cause institutional betrayal trauma (Freyd, Klest, & Allard, 2005; Monteith, Bahraini, Matarazzo, Soberay, & Smith, 2016; Reinhardt, Smith, & Freyd, 2016; Smith, Cunningham, & Freyd, 2016; Smith & Freyd, 2013, 2014). Organizations often betray customers, students, parishioners, prisoners, and others who are not employees, but organizations can also betray their own employees. Kirschman, Kamena, and Fay (2013), for example, described organizational betrayal that many police officers experience. They wrote that when this betrayal occurs, it "complicates traumatic reactions by creating huge doubts about the future" (p. 73) and "makes everything else worse" (p. 57). Surís, Lind, Kashner, and Borman (2007, p. 179; see also Surís, Lind, Kashner, Borman, & Petty, 2004) found that when female soldiers were sexually assaulted within the context of the military organization (i.e., by officers or other military personnel), there were "additional negative consequences above and beyond the effects of [civilian sexual assault]."

To appreciate the ability of such a common event as betrayal to hide out of sight, it may be helpful to remember that psychology itself was slow to recognize it as a topic of study. The PsycNET database includes millions of articles in psychology journals dating back to 1900, but a study—or article of any kind—with the term *betrayal* in the title never appeared in a psychology journal until a single article was published during the 1960s, followed by an average of less than one each year for the next two decades. Finally, in 1992, *Psychotherapy Patient* published 7 articles focusing on betrayal as a special double issue (Volume 8, Issues 3–4), and in 1994, Freyd published "Betrayal Trauma: Traumatic Amnesia as an Adaptive Response to Childhood Abuse," which was followed by Freyd's *Betrayal Trauma: The Logic of Forgetting Childhood Abuse* in 1996. After that, a significant body of published research, theory, and thoughtful discussions began to appear.

Searching out the gaps in an organization can be hard work. We need to develop our ability not only to hunt for them but also to recognize them when we see them. We need to strengthen our talent for noticing. Warren Bennis and Robert Thomas described this talent of effective leaders: "As Saul Bellow says of the character very like himself in his novel *Ravelstein*, they are all 'first-class noticers'" (2002, p. 19).

Sometimes we fail to notice gaps because of cognitive, group, and organizational processes, which are discussed in Chapter 6. Even when we notice a glaring gap, we may hesitate to give voice to it, and when we do speak up, it may do little good, topics discussed in Chapter 7. Sometimes we may not see gaps because of personal blind spots as well as blind spots about our own blind spots. Kahneman reviews research demonstrating "two important facts about our minds: we can be blind to the obvious, and we are also blind to our blindness" (2011, p. 24). And sometimes we fail to see gaps because our eyes are shut tight against seeing what we don't want to see. To notice a particular gap can make us feel afraid that speaking up will bring down disapproval and worse on our heads. To see a gap and keep our mouths shut can make us feel ashamed, guilty, and complicit. And if we are somehow profiting from the gap, we may hate to give up that profit.

This ability to blot out what we don't want to see afflicts us on organizational and individual levels. Margaret Heffernan's research led her to concentrate on intentional blindness on both levels and to recognize "the artificial divide between personal and working lives. Every workforce is a conglomeration of individuals whose behaviors and habits started well before they were hired. Individuals, singly and in groups, are both equally susceptible to willful blindness; what makes organizations different is the sheer scale of damage they can cause" (2011, p. 3).

We must strengthen our ability to notice gaps on both the organizational and individual level, which means we can't let ourselves off the hook. Bennis and Thomas emphasized a trait shared by "all first-class noticers, they observed themselves as well as others" (2002, p. 163). If we open our eyes, do we notice unfortunate gaps between what we say and our actual views, between our words and our actions, between what we believe is "doing the right thing" in a particular situation and what we end up doing?

Beyond our efforts to improve our own individual skills at noticing gaps, making organizational changes can increase the ability of people in the organization to notice. Bazerman (2014) points out that the people who make up organizations often have the skills to notice "but are constrained by the culture or incentive system that exists in their organizations. Leaders should audit their organizations for features that get in the way of noticing" (p. 189).

The following section returns to the case study that runs through this book, showing how even a well-respected organization can, without intending to and almost without noticing, create an unfortunate gap.

Opening a Gap

As described in Chapter 2, in 2015 the American Psychological Association (APA) apologized for causing a "stain on our collective integrity" (McDaniel & Kaslow, 2015c; see also 2015b) and acknowledged that it had begun "resetting our moral compass" (McDaniel & Kaslow, 2015a; see also Aldhaus, 2015, and Wilhelm, 2015). However, the organization had long ago already stepped onto the path that would lead to its current crisis.

Almost a quarter century earlier, APA had, however unintentionally, begun to open up a gap between what had been a code of *professional ethics* but which started to take the form and substance of something quite different: a code of *guild ethics*. *Professional ethics* protect the public against abuse of professional power, expertise, and practice, and hold members accountable to values beyond self-interest. *Guild ethics*, on the other hand, place members' interests above public interest, edge away from accountability, and tend to masquerade as professional ethics. Guild ethics were often associated with trades and crafts rather than professions.

APA took a decisive step onto the path of guild ethics when it adopted the landmark 1992 APA ethics code. Carolyn Payton, who had served on both the APA Policy and Planning Board and the Public Policy Committee, wrote that "all previous codes seemed to have been formulated from a perspective of protecting consumers. The new code appears to be driven by a need to protect psychologists. It reads as though the final draft was edited by lawyers. . . . " (1994, p. 317).

Payton (1994) discussed the "many instances of exceptions to the rule" that would prevent accountability or enforcement:

> The forcefulness of the proscriptions on harassment, e.g., is diminished in . . . Standard 1.12, which brings up the qualifier 'knowingly' . . ., as in psychologists do not knowingly engage in harassment. Try using the argument of ignorance with the Internal Revenue Service.
>
> (p. 320)

Gerry Koocher, who would later serve as APA president, took a similar view: "The code of conduct is disappointing. It is largely reflective of the style of lawyers rather than psychologists and seems more intended to narrow one's liability than to stir one to the highest plane of ethical functioning" (Koocher, 1994, p. 361).

Don Bersoff, who had served as APA's legal counsel and would later serve as its president, wrote that "as almost all the reviewers pointed out, the code is full of such lawyer-driven 'weasel words' as reasonable and feasible" (Bersoff, 1994, p. 384). He summarized a major theme of the reviewers' criticism: "it is a document designed more to protect psychologists than to protect the public" (Bersoff, 1994, p. 383).

APA did not just change its ethics code from protecting the public to protecting psychologists. APA's Ethics Office—which oversees promoting and enforcing APA ethics—no longer concerned itself with protecting the public, the rationale being that public protection was the domain of the state licensing boards. For example, the Director of the Ethics Office from 2000–2015 was quoted by the Special Investigator: "During his interview, he told Sidley that the role of the Ethics Office is not protection of the public and that protection of the public is a function for state licensing boards" (Hoffman et al., 2015, p. 474; see also pp. 11, 63).

Ten years after the landmark 1992 revision, APA further revised its ethics code to reflect an even greater commitment to guild ethics. The organization took a step unprecedented in its over 100-year history, one that was extreme even for guild ethics in protecting members against responsibility or accountability for violating ethics. APA adopted an ethics code (APA, 2002) that abandoned its long-held commitment to the Nuremberg Ethic. The Nuremberg Ethic had seized worldwide attention in the aftermath of World War II. Using what became known as the "Nuremberg Defense," Nazi defendants claimed they held no responsibility for what they had done because they were just "following the law" or "just following orders." The Nuremberg Court and world opinion condemned this excuse for unethical behavior. The court was clear in affirming the Nuremberg Ethic: Those who chose to violate basic ethics could not escape responsibility and accountability by blaming laws, orders, or regulations.

Rejecting the historic Nuremberg Ethic, Section 1.02 of APA's new ethics code stated that when facing an irreconcilable conflict between their "ethical responsibilities" and the state's authority, "psychologists may adhere to the requirements of the law, regulations, or other governing legal authority" (2002). APA discussed and drafted Section 1.02 in the fall of 2000 *before* 9/11 and the "war on terror" (Pope, 2011b; Pope & Gutheil, 2008). However, the military would later emphasize APA's new stance in its policies for psychologists involved in "detention operations, intelligence interrogations, and detainee debriefings" (U.S. Department of the Army, 2006, p. 152). Citing Section 1.02, the army policy stated: "A process for maintaining adherence to the Code when it conflicts with applicable law, regulation, and policy is outlined below" (p. 154). The policy states that after addressing and attempting to resolve the issue, and after appropriate consultation, "If the issue continues to elude resolution, adhere to law, regulations, and policy in a responsible manner."

APA taught and promoted giving greater weight to the U.S government's power and authority—as expressed through laws, orders, or regulations—than to ethics for the next 8 years. For example, the Director of the APA Ethics Office emphasized on a TV/radio news program that "the ethical standards are that psychologists obey the law. Psychologists do not violate the law. . . . The task force states that psychologists have an absolute ethical obligation never to violate any United States law" ("Psychological Warfare?," 2005).

Section 1.02 continued to attract strong criticism even after it had been formal policy for years (e.g., Burton & Kagan, 2007; Godlee, 2009; Kaye, 2008; Levine, 2007; Mausfeld, 2009; Pope & Gutheil, 2009a, 2009b; Soldz, 2009; Tolin & Lohr, 2009; Triskel, 2009). Finally in 2010 APA removed it from the code (APA, 2010).

In the midst of the interrogation and torture controversy, APA adopted and publicized various policies against not only torture (e.g., APA, 2006, 2007, 2008a) but also psychologists working with detainees in violation of international law (APA, 2008b). Questions arose not only about whether there was a giant gap between these policies and APA's (complete lack of) enforcement of them but also about whether some of these policies created a hopeless gap between themselves and any enforcement because the policies themselves were not enforceable. For example, the ballot sent to APA members, through which they banned work with detainees that violated international law (APA, 2008b), included a statement from a former APA president emphasizing APA's stance: "APA is clear that the petition, if adopted, is not enforceable" (Resnick, 2008; see also Pope, 2011a, 2011b).

Assessment for Action

Reflecting on the following questions may be helpful in preparing to strengthen ethics in an organization.

- What gaps, if any, exist between the organization's public image and the reality behind that image?
- Are there gaps between what the organization says and what it does?
- Are there any incentives, aspects of organizational culture, group dynamics, or other factors that get in the way of noticing gaps?
- Are there any incentives, aspects of organizational culture, group dynamics, or other factors that help people in the organization notice gaps?
- Has the organization ever done something (through commission or omission) that could accurately be described as a betrayal? If so, how?
- Has the organization denied or downplayed betrayals and their consequences? If so, how?
- Has the organization failed to assume responsibility for its betrayals?
- What changes would be helpful, and who should design, implement, and monitor them?

Conducting a survey can gather extremely useful information, ideas, and perspectives for addressing these questions. In many organizations, an anonymous survey—one that all respondents accurately believe is truly anonymous—will provide more helpful responses.

References

Aldhaus, P. (2015, August 5). Psychology is in crisis over role in Bush-era torture: At a huge meeting in Toronto, psychologists are grappling with their role in the U.S. government's use of torture; "We've got a fire in our house, and it's a devastating fire," one psychologist told BuzzFeed News. *BuzzFeed News*. Retrieved from www.buzzfeed.com/peteraldhous/psychologists-grapple-with-torture

American Psychological Association. (2002). Ethical principles of psychologists and code of conduct. *American Psychologist, 57,* 1060–1073. http://dx.doi.org/10.1037/0003-066X.57.12.1060

American Psychological Association. (2006). *Resolution against torture and other cruel, inhuman, and degrading treatment or punishment*. Retrieved from www.apa.org/about/policy/torture-2006.aspx

American Psychological Association. (2007). *Reaffirmation of the American Psychological Association position against torture and other cruel, inhuman, or degrading treatment or punishment and its application to individuals defined in the United States code as "enemy combatants."* Retrieved from www.apa.org/about/policy/torture.aspx

American Psychological Association. (2008a). *Amendment to the reaffirmation of the American Psychological Association position against torture.* Retrieved from www.apa.org/about/policy/torture.aspx

American Psychological Association. (2008b). *APA members approve petition resolution on detainee settings* [Press release]. Retrieved from www.apa.org/news/press/releases/2008/09/detainee-petition.aspx

American Psychological Association. (2010). *Ethical principles of psychologists and code of conduct with the 2010 amendments.* Retrieved from http://www.apa.org/ethics/code/index.aspx

Bazerman, M. (2014). *The power of noticing: What the best leaders see* [Kindle for the Mac version]. New York, NY: Simon and Schuster.

Beamish, T. D. (2001). Environmental hazard and institutional betrayal lay-public perceptions of risk in the San Luis Obispo County oil spill. *Organization & Environment, 14*(1), 5–33.

Bennis, W. G., & Thomas, R. J. (2002). *Geeks & geezers: How era, values, and defining moments shape leaders* [Kindle for the Mac version]. Brighton, MA: Harvard Business Press.

Bersoff, D. N. (1994). Explicit ambiguity: The 1992 ethics code as an oxymoron. *Professional Psychology, Research and Practice, 25,* 382–387.

Burton, M., & Kagan, C. (2007). Psychologists and torture: More than a question of interrogation. *The Psychologist, 20,* 484–487.

Cloud, D. S. (2016, December 29). Child abuse in the military: Failing those most in need. *Los Angeles Times.* Retrieved from www.latimes.com/nation/la-na-child-abuse-military-20161229-htmlstory.html

Corkery, M., & Cowley, S. (2016, September 16). Wells Fargo warned workers against sham accounts, but 'they needed a paycheck'. *New York Times.* Retrieved from www.nytimes.com/2016/09/17/business/dealbook/wells-fargo-warned-workers-against-fake-accounts-but-they-needed-a-paycheck.html?hp&action=click&pgtype=Homepage&clickSource=story-heading&module=second-column-region&region=top-news&WT.nav=top-news&_r=0

Cotton, A. (2013, December 5). Argosy University Denver fined $3.3 million for deceptive practices. *Denver Post.* Retrieved from www.denverpost.com/2013/12/05/argosy-university-denver-fined-3-3-million-for-deceptive-practices/

Cowley, S. (2016a, October 20). 'Lions hunting zebras': Ex-Wells Fargo bankers describe abuses. *New York Times.* Retrieved from www.nytimes.com/2016/10/21/business/dealbook/lions-hunting-zebras-ex-wells-fargo-bankers-describe-abuses.html?hp&action=click&pgtype=Homepage&cl

ickSource=story-heading&module=second-column-region&region=top-news&WT.nav=top-news

Cowley, S. (2016b, September 26). Wells Fargo workers claim retaliation for playing by the rules. *New York Times*. Retrieved from www.nytimes.com/2016/09/27/business/dealbook/wells-fargo-workers-claim-retaliation-for-playing-by-the-rules.html?hp&action=click&pgtype=Homepage&clickSource=story-heading&module=first-column-region&region=top-news&WT.nav=top-news

Downe, J., Cowell, R., & Morgan, K. (2016). What determines ethical behavior in public organizations: Is it rules and/or leadership? *Public Administration Review*. Retrieved from http://onlinelibrary.wiley.com/doi/10.1111/puar.12562/full

Freyd, J. (1994). Betrayal trauma: Traumatic amnesia as an adaptive response to childhood abuse. *Ethics & Behavior*, *4*(4), 307–329.

Freyd, J. J. (1996). *Betrayal trauma: The logic of forgetting childhood abuse*. Cambridge, MA: Harvard University Press.

Freyd, J. J., Klest, B., & Allard, C. B. (2005). Betrayal trauma: Relationship to physical health, psychological distress, and a written disclosure intervention. *Journal of Trauma & Dissociation*, *6*(3), 83–104.

Glazer, E. (2016, September 16). How Wells Fargo's high-pressure sales culture spiraled out of control;Hourly targets, fear of being fired and bonuses kept employees selling even when the bank began cracking down on abuses; 'not a team player'. *Wall Street Journal*. Retrieved from www.wsj.com/articles/how-wells-fargos-high-pressure-sales-culture-spiraled-out-of-control-1474053044

Godlee, F. (2009). Rules of conscience. *British Medical Journal*, *338*, 7704. http://dx.doi.org/10.1136/bmj.b1972

Gordon, L. (2015, April 18). UCLA female faculty faced 'demeaning' mistreatment, probe finds. *Los Angeles Times*. Retrieved from www.latimes.com/local/education/la-me-ln-ucla-bias-20150417-story.html

Heffernan, M. (2011). *Wilful blindness: Why we ignore the obvious* [Kindle for the Mac version]. New York, NY: Walker Publishing Company.

Hoffman, D. H., Carter, D. J., Lopez, C. R. V., Benzmiller, H. L., Guo, A. X., Latifi, S. Y., & Craig, D. C. (2015). *Report to the Special Committee of the Board of Directors of the American Psychological Association: Independent review relating to APA Ethics Guidelines, national security interrogations, and torture (revised)*. Chicago, IL: Sidley Austin LLP. Retrieved from www.apa.org/independent-review/revised-report.pdf

Javed, N., & Rushowy, K. (2017, January 20). York trustee apologizes for using racial slur. *Toronto Star*. Retrieved from www.thestar.com/news/gta/2017/01/20/york-trustee-apologizes-for-using-racial-slur.html

Kahneman, D. (2011). *Thinking, fast and slow* [Kindle for the Mac version]. New York, NY: Farrar, Straus and Giroux.

Kaye, J. S. (2008). Why torture made me leave the APA. *Alternet*. Retrieved from www.alternet.org/story/78909/why_torture_made_me_leave_the_apa

Kirschman, E., Kamena, M., & Fay, J. (2013). *Counseling cops: What clinicians need to know*. New York, NY: Guilford Press.

Koehler, J. J., & Gershoff, A. D. (2003). Betrayal aversion: When agents of protection become agents of harm. *Organizational Behavior and Human Decision Processes, 90*(2), 244–261.

Koocher, G. P. (1994). The commerce of professional psychology and the new ethics code. *Professional Psychology, Research and Practice, 25*, 355–361.

Levine, A. (2007, January/February). Collective unconscionable: How psychologists, the most liberal of professionals, abetted Bush's torture policy. *Washington Monthly*. Retrieved from www.washingtonmonthly.com/features/2007/0701.levine.html

Mausfeld, R. (2009). Psychology, "white torture" and the responsibility of scientists. *Psychologische Rundschau, 60*, 229–240. http://dx.doi.org/10.1026/0033-3042.60.4.229

McDaniel, S., & Kaslow, N. (2015a, August 14). *Email message sent by APA President-elect Susan H. McDaniel, PhD, and Past President Nadine J. Kaslow, PhD, ABPP, to all APA members*. Retrieved from www.apa.org/independent-review/member-letter.aspx

McDaniel, S., & Kaslow, N. (2015b, July 24). *Letter to APA members from APA President-Elect Susan McDaniel, PhD, and APA Past President Nadine J. Kaslow, PhD, ABPP, members of the Special Committee for the Independent Review*. Washington, DC: American Psychological Association. Retrieved from www.apa.org/independent-review/letter-members-apology.pdf

McDaniel, S., & Kaslow, N. (2015c, July 21). *Letter to Psychology Colleagues in the International Community from APA President-Elect Susan McDaniel, PhD, and APA Past President Nadine J. Kaslow, PhD, ABPP, members of the Special Committee for the Independent Review*. Washington, DC: American Psychological Association. Retrieved from www.apa.org/independent-review/international-letter.pdf

McDonald's drops nuggets supplier after video shows animal cruelty. (2015, August 27). *The U.K. Guardian*. Retrieved from www.theguardian.com/us-news/2015/aug/27/mcdonalds-drops-chicken-nuggets-supplier-video

Mojica, A. (2015, December 16). Former Ashland City child psychologist sentenced for videos, images of child porn. *Fox 17 Nashville*. Retrieved from http://fox17.com/news/local/former-ashland-city-child-psychologist-sentenced-for-videos-images-of-child-porn

Monteith, L. L., Bahraini, N. H., Matarazzo, B. B., Soberay, K. A., & Smith, C. P. (2016). Perceptions of institutional betrayal predict suicidal self-directed violence among veterans exposed to military sexual trauma. *Journal of Clinical Psychology, 72*(7), 743–755.

Patient gets needless mastectomy after hospital mix-up; Halifax-area hospital authority apologizes as 2 separate mistakes revealed. (2013, August 12). *Canadian Broadcasting Corporation*. Retrieved from www.

cbc.ca/news/canada/nova-scotia/patient-gets-needless-mastectomy-after-hospital-mix-up-1.1353701

Payton, C. R. (1994). Implications of the 1992 ethics code for diverse groups. *Professional Psychology: Research and Practice, 25*(4), 317–320.

Pope, K. S. (2011a). Are the American Psychological Association's detainee interrogation policies ethical and effective? Key claims, documents, and results. *Zeitschrift für Psychologie/The Journal of Psychology, 219*, 150–158. Retrieved from http://bit.ly/APADetaineeInterrogationPolicies

Pope, K. S. (2011b). Psychologists and detainee interrogations: Key decisions, opportunities lost, and lessons learned. *Annual Review of Clinical Psychology, 7*, 459–481. Retrieved from www.annualreviews.org/doi/abs/10.1146/annurev-clinpsy-032210-104612

Pope, K. S., & Gutheil, T. G. (2008). The American Psychological Association & detainee interrogations: Unanswered questions. *Psychiatric Times, 25*, 16–17.

Pope, K. S., & Gutheil, T. G. (2009a). Contrasting ethical policies of physicians and psychologists concerning interrogation of detainees. *British Medical Journal, 338*, b1653. Retrieved from www.bmj.com/content/338/bmj.b1653

Pope, K. S., & Gutheil, T. G. (2009b). Psychologists abandon the Nuremberg ethic: Concerns for detainee interrogations. *International Journal of Law and Psychiatry, 32*, 161–166. http://dx.doi.org/10.1016/j.ijlp.2009.02.005

Psychological warfare? A debate on the role of mental health professionals in military interrogations at Guantanamo, Abu Ghraib and beyond. (2005, August 11). *Democracy Now.* Retrieved from http://bit.ly/ aQ4Azd

Rachman, S. (2010). Betrayal: A psychological analysis. *Behaviour Research and Therapy, 48*(4), 304–311.

Reina, D. S., & Reina, M. L. (2015). *Trust & betrayal in the workplace: Building effective relationships in your organization* (3rd ed.) [Kindle for the Mac version]. Berrett-Koehler Publishers.

Reinhardt, K. M., Smith, C. P., & Freyd, J. J. (2016). Came to serve, left betrayed: Military sexual trauma and the trauma of betrayal. In L. S. Katz (Ed.), *Treating military sexual trauma* (pp. 61–78). New York, NY: Springer.

Resnick, R. J. (2008). *Con statement.* Retrieved from www.apa.org/news/press/statements/work-settings-con.aspx

Roustan, W. K. (2015, August 5). Visiting child psychologist found in Hollywood with child pornography, investigators say. *Sun-Sentinel.* Retrieved from www.sun-sentinel.com/local/broward/fl-child-psychologist-child-porn-20150805-story.html

Scannell, K., & Chon, G. (2015, December 15). Cyber security: Attack of the health hackers. *Financial Times.* Retrieved from xwww.ft.com/content/f3cbda3e-a027-11e5-8613-08e211ea5317#axzz3vA6qRxP8

Slack, D. (2015, September 22). VA watchdog shelves 36,000 complaints, draws ire from whistleblowers. *USA Today.* Retrieved from www.usatoday.com/story/news/nation/2015/09/22/va-watchdog-shelves-36000-complaints-draws-ire-whistleblowers/72643182/

Smith, C. P., Cunningham, S. A., & Freyd, J. J. (2016). Sexual violence, institutional betrayal, and psychological outcomes for LGB college students. *Translational Issues in Psychological Science, 2*(4), 351–360.

Smith, C. P., & Freyd, J. J. (2013). Dangerous safe havens: Institutional betrayal exacerbates sexual trauma. *Journal of Traumatic Stress, 26*(1), 119–124.

Smith, C. P., & Freyd, J. J. (2014). Institutional betrayal. *American Psychologist, 69*(6), 575.

Soldz, S. (2009, July 27). Will the American Psychological Association renounce the Nuremberg defense? *Counterpunch.* Retrieved from www.counterpunch.org/2009/07/27/will-the-american-psychological-association-renounce-the-nuremberg-defense/

Surís, A., Lind, L., Kashner, T. M., & Borman, P. D. (2007). Mental health, quality of life, and health functioning in women veterans: Differential outcomes associated with military and civilian sexual assault. *Journal of Interpersonal Violence, 22*(2), 179–197.

Surís, A., Lind, L., Kashner, T. M., Borman, P. D., & Petty, F. (2004). Sexual assault in women veterans: An examination of PTSD risk, health care utilization, and cost of care. *Psychosomatic Medicine, 66,* 749–756.

Tolin, D. F., & Lohr, J. M. (2009). Psychologists, the APA, and torture. *Clinical Science Newsletter, 12,* 4–10.

Triskel, N. (2009). Fortunately UK psychologists don't use the APA code of ethics. *British Medical Journal.* Retrieved from www.bmj.com/rapid-response/2011/11/02/fortunately-uk-psychologists-dont-use-apa-code-ethics

Ulmer, W. (1970). *Study on military professionalism.* Carlisle Barracks, PA: US Army War College.

U.S. Department of the Army. (2006). *Behavioral science consultation policy.* Washington, DC: Author.

Viscusi, W. K. (2015, May). Pricing lives for corporate risk decisions. *Vanderbilt Law Review,* 14–26.

Waldman, A., & Ornstein, C. (2015, December 30). Another VA headache: Privacy violations rising at Veterans' Medical Facilities. *Pro Publica.* Retrieved from http://bit.ly/1ZCdvDN

Wilhelm, I. (2015). Meeting of psychologists becomes a moment of soul searching. *Chronicle of Higher Education.* Retrieved from http://chronicle.com/article/A-Meeting-of-Psychologists/232267

Zoltners, A., Sinha, P., & Lorimer, S. (2016, September 20). Wells Fargo and the slippery slope of sales incentives. *Harvard Business Review.* Retrieved from https://hbr.org/2016/09/wells-fargo-and-the-slippery-slope-of-sales-incentives

5   Waking the Watchdogs

Overcoming Silence and Gaining Strength From Critics, Whistleblowers, and Bearers of Bad News

Chapters 3 and 4 suggest anonymous surveys as one way to gather information to strengthen ethics in an organization and the individuals within it. Why? Because people in the organization often keep their mouths shut tight—at least publicly or when speaking to those in power—about concerns that something is not quite right, headed for disaster, or already in meltdown. They may believe or suspect that the organization's direction, values, culture, code, code enforcement, or practices need rethinking and yet not breathe a word of this to anyone in the organization who has power to do something about it or at least turn the organization's attention to it.

Silence in Organizations and Its Causes

Research suggests that this selective silence falls over many organizations. Milliken, Morrison, and Hewlin (2003), for example, found that "85 per cent of our sample [reported] that, on at least one occasion, they had felt unable to raise an issue or concern to their bosses even though they felt the issue was important" (p. 1459). Maxfield (2016) cited both a study of healthcare organizations in which "we found that 90% of nurses don't speak up to a physician even when they know a patient's safety is at risk" and also a study of workplace safety in organizations in which "we found that 93% of people say their organization is at risk of an accident waiting to happen because people are either unwilling or unable to speak up." Morrison reviewed the research and found that it supported the idea that "silence is not an uncommon choice in the workplace" (2014, p. 178).

Does this ring true for any organizations you've been a part of? Have you or others hesitated to speak up? Did unwritten rules encourage people to remain silent about certain topics or events? How likely was it that everyone felt free to point out mistakes, raise concerns, or challenge the rightness of policies to the head of the organization, a supervisor, or others in power? Was the fact of the silence itself ever discussed among some members of the organization or was mentioning the silence off-limits?

One of the best-known Sherlock Holmes stories tells of how the midnight theft of a horse has baffled everyone. Holmes solves the case when he realizes that the watchdog had remained silent during the theft "and obviously the midnight visitor was someone the dog knew well" (Doyle, 1892/2004, p. 334). When we work to strengthen ethics in an organization and the individuals who are a part of it, we face the challenge of finding out if the ethical watchdogs are keeping quiet when they should be waking up the organization. Organizations often look to a committee, department, or individual as the "watchdog," but the responsibility to wake the organization to actual or potential failures to do the right thing, to ethical questions and concerns, is best shared by everyone and works best when everyone feels not just free to speak up but responsible for speaking up.

Why the silence? Keeping quiet makes great sense from the point of view of those who keep quiet. Kish-Gephart, Detert, Treviño, and Edmondson (2009) wrote, "In every organization, individual members have the potential to speak up about important issues, but a growing body of research suggests that they often remain silent instead, out of fear of negative personal and professional consequences" (p. 163; see also Milliken, Morrison, & Hewlin, 2003). Detert and Treviño (2010) noted that many employees believe from the time they set foot in the door that part of their organizational role is to "'tread lightly' around those in power" (p. 264). The unspoken rules in many organizations, as summarized by Jackall (1988), are hard to miss even for new arrivals:

> You never go around your boss. . . . You tell your boss what he wants to hear, even when your boss claims that he wants dissenting views. . . . If your boss wants something dropped, you drop it. . . . You do what your job requires, and you keep your mouth shut.
>
> (p. 115)

Fear is not the only factor fostering silence in organizations. Another of the personal, group, cultural, or organizational factors is a sense of hopelessness and helplessness. Members of the organization may believe that speaking up will accomplish nothing. Pinder and Harlos describe acquiescent silence (see also Bormann & Rowold, 2016; Dedahanov, Kim, & Rhee, 2015; Harlos, 2016):

> Acquiescence is a deeper state of silence. . . . Acquiescent employees are less conscious of their silence. . . . People in deep acquiescence have given up hope of improvement and become more or less oblivious to the importance of external events that may provide grounds for hope and a possibility for amelioration.
>
> (2001, p. 349)

Whistleblowers and What Happens to Them

Deciding whether to break through a wall of silence and speak up about serious problems when others are busy keeping their mouths shut weighs heavily on most potential whistleblowers. Research suggests that whistleblowers must overcome fears that they will face retaliation or that the risks they take will all be for nothing (Mayer, Nurmohamed, Treviño, Shapiro, & Schminke, 2013; Mesmer-Magnus & Viswesvaran, 2005; Miceli, Near, & Dworkin, 2013). In a survey in which 1,366 actual whistleblowers participated, the most common reason given for waiting to report wrongdoing internally (i.e., to people within the organization) was "I feared reprisal" (Government Accountability Project, 2016, p. 10) and the third most common response was fear that "nothing would be done if I came forward" (p. 10). (The second most common reason for delaying was to gather more evidence or gain a better understanding to back up allegations of wrongdoing.)

Whistleblowers' fears that they will suffer punishment for speaking up and that it will all come to nothing anyway are often an accurate reading of reality. Dyer (2014), for example, reported that "more than half the whistleblowers who contacted the UK charity Public Concern at Work for advice in 2012 were sacked or resigned after raising concerns about wrongdoing, risk, or malpractice" (p. 6285). An additional 22% were disciplined or punished in other ways. Only 6% reported that their speaking up led to improvements in the workplace.

Rothschild and Miethe (1999) found that whistleblowers tend to "suffer severe retaliation from management, especially when their information proves significant" (p. 107). McDonald and Ahern (2000) found that nurse whistleblowers tended to suffer severe consequences and that nurses who kept their mouths shut experienced few negative effects. Some of the consequences for those who spoke up were:

> demotion (4%), reprimand (11%), and referral to a psychiatrist (9%). Whistleblowers also reported [receiving] professional reprisals in the form of threats (16%), rejection by peers (14%), pressure to resign (7%), and being treated as a traitor (14%). Ten per cent reported that they felt their career had been halted.
> (McDonald & Ahern, 2000, p. 313)

Sherron Watkins (2013), formerly of Enron, described how blowing the whistle on questionable activities can wreck a career. The media provided positive coverage of her insider disclosures of Enron's wrongdoing and her testifying as a key prosecution witness in the criminal and civil trials. She shared the cover of *Time* with two other whistleblowers from other organizations as *Time*'s "Person of the Year." The corporate world, however, wanted nothing to do with her. A decade later she wrote that "the label Enron whistleblower means I will not work in Corporate America again" (p. ix).

A Case Study

The case study described in detail in Chapter 2 illustrates how speaking up can be met with attempts to disparage and discredit the speaker. For example, the American Association for the Advancement of Science (AAAS) honored APA member Jean Maria Arrigo, one who spoke up, with the AAAS Scientific Freedom and Responsibility Award because she "confronted systematic efforts by the American Psychological Association (APA) to allow and conceal the involvement of psychologists in the torture and abuse of detainees" (Korke, 2016). Yet a newspaper reporter documented how she had been "largely ignored and the subject of a smear campaign for sounding alarms about psychologists' post-9/11 torture complicity" (Ackerman, 2015). The investigation and final report commissioned by APA itself found that she was subjected to "a highly personal attack" (Hoffman et al., 2015). APA later formally acknowledged that this whistleblower faced not only "efforts to discredit, isolate, and shun" that were "orchestrated movements by those in positions of power" but also "harsh, hostile personal criticism and attacks" (Watt, 2015). For additional examples of efforts to disparage, discredit, and discount those inside and outside (both individuals and groups such as the International Committee of the Red Cross, human rights organizations, and the Department of Defense Inspector General) who voiced evidence and arguments running contrary to APA's stance, see Pope (2011a, 2011b, 2016).

Breaking the Silence

Freeing the organization from a culture of silence means creating a shared sense of psychological safety in the workgroups, departments, offices, and throughout all levels of the organization. Most of us are reluctant to speak up if we believe our ideas will be instantly shot down and that we will be the targets of discounting, disparagement, or retaliation.

Psychological safety is the sense that we are safe when we take risks (Edmondson, 1999; Newman, Donohue, & Eva, 2017). Edmondson and Lei reviewed the research and found that "studies show that individuals who experience greater psychological safety are more likely to speak up at work." They also found that although speaking up to challenge what is currently going on in an organization, point out problems, and so on, "can feel risky," research findings on psychological safety "suggests that mitigating this risk is possible" (2014, p. 37).

Leadership plays a key role in creating a sense of psychological safety and a culture that supports people speaking up. Research by Walumbwa and Schaubroeck (2009), for example, found "that ethical leadership has substantial effects on psychological safety and voice behavior" (p. 1283; see also Hsiung, 2012; Ortega, Van den Bossche, Sanchez-Manzanares, Rico, & Gil, 2014; Tangirala & Ramanujam, 2012; Wong, Laschinger, & Cummings, 2010).

The history of the New United Motors Manufacturing Corporation (NUMMI) shows the challenges leadership can face in creating a culture in which members of the organization are willing to break the silence when there's a problem. The GM plant in Freemont, California, was a nightmare: "It was a highly developed example of everything that could be wrong with American management. Absenteeism was raging at about 20%. The union had about 800 grievances pending. Quality and productivity were abysmal. Drug and alcohol abuse were rampant. Fights would break out on the floor" (Holden, 1986, p. 273). GM closed the plant in 1982, but it came to life again as a cooperative venture of two competitors: GM and Toyota. The Federal Trade Commission authorized GM and Toyota to reopen the plant as a joint-venture under a new corporation—the New United Motors

Manufacturing Corporation—for 12 years. GM gave Toyota operational control to see if principles developed in its Japanese plants could be successful with workers who grew up in the U.S. system (Monden, 2011; Rother, 2010; Shook, 2010).

Toyota worked with the United Automobile Workers union to hire back many who had worked in the old plant. When the NUMMI plant reopened in December 1984, "99 percent of the production workers and 75 percent of the skilled trades workers were former GM-Fremont employees" (Adler, Goldoftas, & Levine, 1998, p. 130). These workers were used to a system in which the prime directive was keeping the assembly line going at all costs. The old plant had often put out cars riddled with defects in part because workers knew that the biggest sin was stopping the assembly line to fix something. Each minute the assembly line failed to move could cost the company up to $15,000 (Duhigg, 2016). Line workers themselves were not even allowed to stop the line. They feared putting their supervisors, who could stop the line, on the spot by pointing out problems. No one wanted to be blamed—and perhaps fired—for bringing everything to a stop, costing the plant precious minutes and thousands of dollars.

Toyota tried to change this culture. To produce error-free cars, everyone had to be on the lookout for defects *and* make sure others knew about them so that they could be fixed, even if that meant stopping the line. Essential to the process was that each worker had not only the power but also the responsibility for calling attention to problems (Monden, 2011). The new culture gave every line worker responsibility for making sure defects were identified, even if it meant stopping the line. The new culture also gave each line worker an andon cord to pull whenever a worker could not fix a problem quickly.

Extensive training emphasized that each worker had not only the right but also the responsibility to pull the andon cord when spotting a problem. Pulling the andon cord turned on a yellow light that could be seen by everyone and alerted the supervisor, who immediately: (a) thanked the worker for identifying the problem, and (b) asked the worker what help was needed (Monden, 2011; Rother, 2010). If the problem was not solved within one minute, the light turned red and the line stopped.

The training seemed to have no effect. No one wanted to pull the andon cord. Duhigg (2016) describes the turning point. A few weeks after the plant reopened, Tetsuro Toyoda, NUMMI's president and grandson of the man who had founded Toyota, noticed a worker named Joe struggling unsuccessfully to fix a taillight. Toyoda asked Joe to pull the cord, but Joe wanted to avoid pulling the cord at all costs—he had never pulled the cord and was terrified—and assured Toyoda he could take care of it. Toyoda asked again, as the other line workers and supervisors looked on. Finally, Toyoda leaned over, gently took Joe's hand, placed it around the andon cord, and pulled it. The yellow light had turned to red before Joe was able to fix the taillight and pull the cord again to start the line moving again.

Toyoda waited until he and Joe were facing each other. Then he bowed and said:

> Joe, please forgive me. . . . I have done a poor job of instructing your managers of the importance of helping you pull the cord when there is a problem. You are the most important part of this plant. . . . I will do everything in my power to never fail you again.
>
> (Duhigg, 2016)

This event shattered the taboo and helped change the culture. Before long each day brought around 100 pulls on the andon cord.

Strengthening ethics in an organization and the individuals who make up the organization includes creating a culture of psychological safety in which each person throughout the organization not only receives encouragement and support in raising ethical questions and concerns but also shoulders the personal responsibility for speaking up when there's a problem.

Assessment for Action

The following questions may be helpful when thinking through ways to strengthen ethics in an organization and the individuals who make up the organization.

- How often do people speak up about ethical problems, questions, or concerns?
- What happens when they do?
- Are there any topics that seem to be off-limits?
- Are there any particular workgroups, offices, departments, or other parts of the organization in which there seems to be a reluctance to speak up?
- What factors seem to contribute to the silence?
- Are there any workgroups, offices, departments, or other parts of the organization which seem to lack an adequate sense of psychological safety?

- How do leaders address issues of silence, voice, and psychological safety?
- In what ways, if any, does the organization encourage and support a sense of personal responsibility for speaking up among all members of the organization?
- Has there ever been a need for a whistleblower? If so, did one or more people blow the whistle? What happened to them and to whatever caused them to blow the whistle?

A culture of silence and silencing can close off many routes to better organizational ethics. An anonymous survey might begin by asking individuals in the organization the following: If you were to raise concerns about ethics or blow the whistle on unethical behavior, how do you think your colleagues and those higher up in the organization would respond, what would happen to your concerns, and what would happen to you?

But if the organization's culture lacks trust, those asked to fill out the survey may wonder: Will they recognize my identity in some way? Are the forms coded? If I go to all the trouble of filling it out, will anyone even read it? Take it seriously? Treat it fairly? Use it to make things better? In some cases, it may make more sense to simply start looking for ways to change the culture and dynamics of silencing. What immediate steps would encourage and support speaking up and show that valid criticism is heard, valued, and acted on with fairness and justice? Can the costs of speaking up be eliminated or at least minimized?

References

Ackerman, S. (2015, July 13). 'A national hero': Psychologist who warned of torture collusion gets her due. *The Guardian*. Retrieved from http://bit.ly/2lPSg3M

Adler, P. S., Goldoftas, B., & Levine, D. I. (1998). Stability and change at NUMMI. In R. Boyer, E. Charron, U. Jurgens, & S. Tolliday (Eds.), *Between imitation and innovation, the transfer and hybridization of productive models in the international automobile industry* (pp. 128–161). New York, NY: Oxford University Press.

Bormann, K. C., & Rowold, J. (2016). Ethical leadership's potential and boundaries in organizational change: A moderated mediation model of employee silence. *Zeitschrift fur Personalforschung, 30*(3–4), 225–245.

Dedahanov, A. T., Kim, C., & Rhee, J. (2015). Centralization and communication opportunities as predictors of acquiescent or prosocial silence. *Social Behavior and Personality, 43*(3), 481–492.

Detert, J. R., & Treviño, L. K. (2010). Speaking up to higher-ups: How super-visors and skip-level leaders influence employee voice. *Organization Science, 21*(1), 249–270.

Doyle, A. C. (2004). Silver blaze. In *The adventures and the memoirs of Sherlock Holmes* (pp. 311–336). New York, NY: Sterling Publishing Company. (Originally published 1892)

Duhigg, C. (2016). *Smarter faster better* [Kindle for the Mac version]. New York, NY: Random House.

Dyer, C. (2014). Half of whistleblowers who raised work concerns with charity were sacked or resigned. *BMJ, 349*, g6285.

Edmondson, A. (1999). Psychological safety and learning behavior in work teams. *Administrative Science Quarterly, 44*(2), 350–383.

Edmondson, A. C., & Lei, Z. (2014). Psychological safety: The history, renaissance, and future of an interpersonal construct. *Annual Review of Organizational Psychology and Organizational Behavior, 1*(1), 23–43.

Government Accountability Project. (2016). *Why whistleblowers wait.* Washington, DC: Author.

Harlos, K. (2016). Employee silence in the context of unethical behavior at work: A commentary. *Zeitschrift fur Personalforschung, 30*(3–4), 345–355.

Hoffman, D. H., Carter, D. J., Lopez, C. R. V., Benzmiller, H. L., Guo, A. X., Latifi, S. Y., & Craig, D. C. (2015). *Report to the Special Committee of the Board of Directors of the American Psychological Association: Independent review relating to APA Ethics Guidelines, national security interrogations, and torture (revised).* Chicago, IL: Sidley Austin LLP. Retrieved from www.apa.org/independent-review/revised-report.pdf

Holden, C. (1986). New Toyota-GM plant is US model for Japanese management. *Science, 233*, 273–278.

Hsiung, H.-H. (2012). Authentic leadership and employee voice behavior: A multi-level psychological process. *Journal of Business Ethics, 107*(3), 349–361.

Jackall, R. (1988). *Moral mazes: The world of corporate managers.* New York, NY: Oxford University Press.

Kish-Gephart, J. J., Detert, J. R., Treviño, L. K., & Edmondson, A. C. (2009). Silenced by fear: The nature, sources, and consequences of fear at work. *Research in Organizational Behavior, 29*, 163–193.

Korke, A. (2016, February 8). 2015 AAAS scientific freedom and responsibility award goes to social psychologist Jean Maria Arrigo. *American Association for the Advancement of Science.* Retrieved from http://bit.ly/2kqMR6e

Maxfield, D. (2016, December 7). How a culture of silence eats away at your company. *Harvard Business Review.* Retrieved from https://hbr.org/2016/12/how-a-culture-of-silence-eats-away-at-your-company

Mayer, D. M., Nurmohamed, S., Treviño, L. K., Shapiro, D. L., & Schminke, M. (2013). Encouraging employees to report unethical conduct internally: It takes a village. *Organizational Behavior and Human Decision Processes, 121*(1), 89–103.

McDonald, S., & Ahern, K. (2000). The professional consequences of whistle-blowing by nurses. *Journal of Professional Nursing, 16*(6), 313–321.

Mesmer-Magnus, J. R., & Viswesvaran, C. (2005). Whistleblowing in organizations: An examination of correlates of whistleblowing intentions, actions, and retaliation. *Journal of Business Ethics, 62*(3), 277–297.

Miceli, M. P., Near, J. P., & Dworkin, T. M. (2013). *Whistle-blowing in organizations*. New York, NY: Taylor & Francis.

Milliken, F. J., Morrison, E. W., & Hewlin, P. F. (2003). An exploratory study of employee silence: Issues that employees don't communicate upward and why. *Journal of Management Studies, 40*(6), 1453–1476.

Monden, Y. (2011). *Toyota production system: An integrated approach to just-in-time* (4th ed.) [Kindle for the Mac version]. Boca Raton, FL: CRC Press.

Newman, A., Donohue, R., & Eva, N. (2017, January). Psychological safety: A systematic review of the literature. *Human Resource Management Review*, pp. 1–15.

Ortega, A., Van den Bossche, P., Sanchez-Manzanares, M., Rico, R., & Gil, F. (2014). The influence of change-oriented leadership and psychological safety on team learning in healthcare teams. *Journal of Business and Psychology, 29*(2), 311–321.

Pinder, C. C., & Harlos, K. P. (2001). Employee silence: Quiescence and acquiescence as responses to perceived injustice. In M. Ronald Buckley, J. R. B. Halbesleben, & A. R. Wheeler (Eds.), *Research in personnel and human resources management* (pp. 331–369). Bingley, UK: Emerald Group Publishing Limited.

Pope, K. S. (2011a). Are the American Psychological Association's detainee interrogation policies ethical and effective? Key claims, documents, and results. *Zeitschrift für Psychologie/The Journal of Psychology, 219*, 150–158. Retrieved from http://bit.ly/APADetaineeInterrogationPolicies

Pope, K. S. (2011b). Psychologists and detainee interrogations: Key decisions, opportunities lost, and lessons learned. *Annual Review of Clinical Psychology, 7*, 459–481. Retrieved from www.annualreviews.org/doi/abs/10.1146/annurev-clinpsy-032210-104612

Pope, K. S. (2016). The Code Not Taken: The Path From Guild Ethics to Torture and Our Continuing Choices—Canadian Psychological Association Member of the Year Award Address. *Canadian Psychology/Psychologie Canadienne, 57*(1), 51–59.

Rother, M. (2010). *Toyota kata*. New York, NY: McGraw-Hill.

Rothschild, J., & Miethe, T. D. (1999). Whistle-blower disclosures and management retaliation: The battle to control information about organization corruption. *Work and Occupations, 26*(1), 107–128.

Shook, J. (2010, Winter). How to change a culture: Lessons from NUMMI. *MIT Sloan Management Review*. Retrieved from http://sloanreview.mit.edu/article/how-to-change-a-culture-lessons-from-nummi

Tangirala, S., & Ramanujam, R. (2012). Ask and you shall hear (but not always): Examining the relationship between manager consultation and employee voice. *Personnel Psychology, 65*(2), 251–282.

Walumbwa, F. O., & Schaubroeck, J. (2009). Leader personality traits and employee voice behavior: Mediating roles of ethical leadership and work group psychological safety. *Journal of Applied Psychology, 94*(5), 1275–1286.

Watkins, S. S. (2013). Foreword. In S. V. Arbogast (Ed.), *Resisting corporate corruption: Cases in practical ethics from Enron through the financial crisis* (pp. ix–xii). New York, NY: Wiley.

Watt, S. M. (2015, August 10). Psychologists honor anti-torture whistle-blower. *ACLU*. Retrieved from http://bit.ly/2lPWsRd

Wong, C. A., Laschinger, H. K., & Cummings, G. G. (2010). Authentic leadership and nurses' voice behaviour and perceptions of care quality. *Journal of Nursing Management, 18*(8), 889–900.

6 Recognizing and Avoiding Common Stumbles Over Heuristics and Other Sources of Bias

We may have gone over our plans to strengthen ethics in organizations and the individuals who make up the organization a thousand times—or at least two or three times—to assure ourselves that they are perfectly rational. And yet . . . Too many sets of perfectly rational plans wander slowly or run headlong into trouble because they don't take account of one obvious but often underestimated truth: Neither the people trying to implement the plans nor other individuals who make up the organization act like purely rational beings. Unrealistic plans treat people as if they were computers programmed to reason perfectly and to behave following the rules of rationality.

Our minds often follow nonrational rules.

> Nearly all of these rules prefer simplicity over rationality, and many even contradict each other. Those that are not quite rational but perhaps not a bad rule of thumb are called "heuristics." Those that utterly fly in the face of reason are called "fallacies."
>
> (Hubbard, 2014, p. 307)

This chapter is a reminder of 7 heuristics and other human tendencies that seem most often to baffle and break the best laid plans. Taking this 4th step to make sure we take account of these tendencies can help keep us on a productive path.

The Planning Fallacy and Optimistic Bias

Plans can dazzle us with their detailed designs, their compelling logic, their reassuring simplicity: We know what we're going to do, how we're going to do it, about how long it will take, and what the pay-off will be for all our work. Just when we're feeling supremely confident is likely when we are held tight in the grip of optimistic bias and one of its most debilitating symptoms, the planning fallacy. We know how we *want* things to go and we expect them to go pretty much as we want them to.

To focus on just one specific aspect of this fallacy: We tend to underestimate how long it will take to complete a project. Buehler and Griffin (2003) found that the optimistic bias about how long a project will take occurs not just with optimistic people but also others, with different kinds of tasks, and in different contexts.

But the optimistic bias extends far beyond estimating the time we'll need to carry out our plans. Lench and his colleagues wrote that it is a human tendency for us to think that what will happen in the future will match up well with what we want to happen, and that we think that we:

> are likely to experience desirable events and unlikely to experience undesirable events. This desirability bias in judgment has been demonstrated across populations, with a variety of methodologies, and for numerous events (sometimes termed optimistic bias, wishful thinking, or illusion of invulnerability).
>
> (Lench, Smallman, & Berg, 2016; see also
> Klein & Helweg-Larsen, 2002)

Kahneman emphasized the wide scope of optimistic bias, describing how most of us see:

> the world as more benign than it really is, our own attributes as more favorable than they truly are, and the goals we adopt as more achievable than they are likely to be. We also tend to exaggerate our ability to forecast the future, which fosters optimistic overconfidence.
>
> (Kahneman, 2011, p. 255)

He believes that the optimistic bias is likely the most serious cognitive bias because of its effects on our decisions.

The challenge in confronting this bias is to try to build into our plans all the "worst possible case" scenarios—complications affecting the organization (e.g., changes in leadership, financial shortfalls, mergers, a crisis), reactions to the plans themselves (institutional inertia, active resistance), and ourselves (illness, family emergency, financial shortfalls)—without losing our enthusiasm, determination, and confidence that we can get the job done.

The Bias of Illusory Ethical Superiority

When we try to take a good hard look at our own ethics and moral qualities, most of us are shamelessly easy graders. We grade on a curve and bend the curve so that it puts us higher than others. As early as 2000, Epley and Dunning (see also Allison, Messick, & Goethals, 1989; Brown, 1986; Heck & Krueger, 2016; Hess, Cossette, & Hareli, 2016; Messick, Bloom, Boldizar, & Samuelson, 1985) pointed out that

> researchers have repeatedly demonstrated that people on average tend to think they are more charitable, cooperative, considerate, fair, kind, loyal, and sincere than the typical person but less belligerent, deceitful, gullible, lazy, impolite, mean, and unethical—just to name a few.
>
> (2000, p. 861)

Although we may have a biased view of ourselves in many areas, the bias of ethical arrogance seems more extreme. Tappin and McKay (2016), for example, found that "the belief that one is morally superior to the average person appears robust and widespread. Our examination of this belief revealed substantial irrationality beyond that observed in other domains of positive self-evaluation. On this basis, moral superiority represents a uniquely strong and prevalent form of positive illusion."

This common human tendency to believe in the illusion of our own ethical superiority, when shared by the people who make up an organization, creates a barrier to strengthening ethics in the organization and its members. It throws us off course before we even get started. It blocks us from a realistic view of the organization's ethics. Why, after all, waste our time and scarce resources trying to strengthen organizational ethics when the ethics of the organization and its members are already strong and significantly superior compared to others?

This common human tendency can also drain the effectiveness of anyone trying to make organizational ethics stronger. If we fall prey to the bias of illusory ethical superiority, we can come across as arrogant, holier-than-thou know-it-alls. The walls immediately go up against anything we have to say. Does anyone within or outside an organization seek out an arrogant, holier-than-thou know-it-all for ethical guidance? Does anyone within or outside an organization tend to listen to an arrogant, holier-than-thou know-it-all? When any of us is approached by an arrogant, holier-than-thou know-it-all, are we caught between an impulse to run and a desperate hope that this, like a bad case of the flu, will pass as quickly as possible, if not sooner?

Mindlessness and Disengagement

Mindlessness and disengagement reflect the mind's tendency to wander, to flee, or to snooze when it should be fully awake and aware of the matter at hand. In her book *Mindfulness*, Ellen Langer (2014) reviews research showing how easily we slip into a mindless state through habit, repetition, and familiarity. She describes one study in which she and her colleagues delivered interdepartmental memos that said simply "Please return this immediately to Room 247" or "This memo is to be returned to Room 247" to offices around the university (Langer, 2014, p. 16). If someone read the memo mindfully, it would be clear the memo made no sense at all. If the *only* goal was for the memo to be in Room 247, why would the author send it out from Room 247, asking that it be returned? Half of the memos looked exactly like those currently in use at the university. They were familiar to the recipients, who were in the habit of handling these sorts of memos. A surprising 90% of the recipients followed the instructions and completed the meaningless task of returning these memos to Room 247. The other half of the memos looked just a bit different from those the recipients were used to. Nevertheless, 60% of the recipients complied with the pointless instructions. Langer surveys research and case studies showing that the "consequences of mindlessness range from the trivial to the catastrophic" (p. 46).

The antidote to mindlessness is staying awake at the switch: paying close attention to our work and its ethical implications, broadening our scope, taking a new look at "the way we've always done it," considering alternatives, constantly questioning, and making good use of the word "why." It may be useful to remind ourselves of the dangers of mindlessly drifting toward detachment from the ethical implications of what we are doing. Bandura (1990) describes how easy it is for most of us, if our minds are not awake and aware, to slide into a deep state of moral disengagement (see also Aquino, Reed, Thau, & Freeman, 2007; Bandura, Caprara, Barbaranelli, Pastorelli, & Regalia, 2001; McAlister, Bandura, & Owen, 2006; Moore, 2008; Osofsky, Bandura, & Zimbardo, 2005). We start the descent by mindlessly repeating mildly questionable acts:

> Initially, individuals are prompted to perform questionable acts that they can tolerate with little self-censure. After their

discomfort and self-reproof have been diminished through repeated performances, the level of reprehensibility progressively increases until, eventually, acts originally regarded as abhorrent can be performed without much distress.

(Bandura, 1990, p. 42)

Research in both the lab and the field suggests that our tendency to slip into moral disengagement is predictive of such outcomes as self-reported unethical behavior, the choice to engage in fraud, workplace decisions that are self-serving, reduced prosocialness, and unethical behaviors at work as reported by supervisors and coworkers (Bandura, 2016; Detert, Treviño, & Sweitzer, 2008; Moore et al., 2012).

Moral disengagement allows us to continue to think well of ourselves while engaging in unethical behavior. We don't even need to change our moral standards. It gives people who are morally disengaged a way "to circumvent moral standards in ways that strip morality from harmful behavior and their responsibility for it. However, in other aspects of their lives, they adhere to their moral standards" (Bandura, 2016, p. 2).

Confirmation Bias

We love to think of ourselves as open to new information and ideas, weighing them carefully and fairly. Unfortunately we tend to notice and seek out whatever supports our current assumptions, beliefs, and theories, and to filter out evidence that challenges our views. Recognition of this bias toward confirming evidence and the ways it can throw us off course reaches back centuries. Francis Bacon wrote in 1620 that once we have formed an opinion about something, our minds gather material:

> to support and agree with it. And though there be a greater number and weight of instances to be found on the other side, yet these it either neglects or despises, or else by some distinction sets aside and rejects . . . This mischief insinuate[s] itself into philosophy and the sciences . . .
>
> (1955, p. 472)

Recognition of the power of confirmation bias when it has us in its grip also reaches far back into the past. In 1841, MacKay (2009) wrote: "When men wish to construct or support a theory, how they torture facts into their service!"

Confirmation bias plays a role in areas as diverse as EMG research (Narayanaswami et al., 2016), politics (Knobloch-Westerwick, Mothes,

Johnson, Westerwick, & Donsbach, 2015), aviation (Gilbey & Hill, 2012; Walmsley & Gilbey, 2016), diagnosis (Langer, 2014; Mendel et al., 2011), and forensic science (Kassin, Dror, & Kukucka, 2013; Kukucka, J., & Kassin, 2014; Richards, Geiger, & Tussey, 2015). This bias colors our thinking so often that Nickerson (1998), in his review of the research, called confirmation bias "a ubiquitous phenomenon in many guises" (p. 175).

Confirmation bias freezes us in place, shutting out information that could cause us to move from our familiar and often heavily guarded positions. If we believe our organization is already ethically strong, it can be hard to see flaws, lapses, and red flags. If we're sure that we already know where the weaknesses are, we may ignore areas in much greater need of attention. If we've found the perfect plan for strengthening ethics in the organization, we may not listen to people inside and outside the organization who could show us how to improve our plan or even convince us to toss it aside and start over. Reviewing the research, Lilienfeld (2015) reminds us that "many of the most disastrous errors in (a) the history of science, including psychological science and (b) psychological and medical treatments stem from the failure to confront the perils posed by confirmation bias."

GroupThink

For all their rich resources and benefits, groups pose a major risk when we're thinking through how to approach an ethical dilemma, or how to strengthen ethics in organizations and individuals, or what to do in . . . almost any other situation. GroupThink puts our minds on autopilot. We can lean back and stop thinking things through, stop questioning, stop considering other viewpoints and possibilities. Some idea grips the group and we all get on board. GroupThink gives us false confidence. After all, *everyone* in the group thinks the decision, plan, or action is right. Or at least no one in the group is speaking up to say it's wrong, or even to raise questions or concerns, or to suggest we're going too fast. GroupThink can drain our sense of individual responsibility. It is as if some organism known as The Group—but no individual member of that group—is responsible for decisions and actions.

In his article "Why I Do Not Attend Case Conferences," psychologist Paul Meehl (1973/1977) described the "groupthink process" (p. 228) in ways that, unfortunately, may be familiar to many of us:

> In one respect the clinical case conference is no different from other academic group phenomena such as committee meetings,

in that many intelligent, educated, sane, rational persons seem to undergo a kind of intellectual deterioration when they gather around a table in one room.

(p. 227)

Meehl's use of the term "deterioration" echoes the description used by psychologist Irving Janis, who originally developed the concept of GroupThink, describing it as "a deterioration of mental efficiency, reality testing, and moral judgment that results from in-group pressures" (1982a, p. 9; see also Janis, 1972, 1982b). Janis and Mann (1977, pp. 103–131) flagged 8 key symptoms of GroupThink, which are paraphrased and adapted (to the theme of this book) below, that we should look out for in our work in and with groups.

- As a group, we feel invulnerable and recklessly optimistic, as if nothing could go wrong. We're ready, without real justification or even careful thought, to take on even extreme risks.
- We quickly bat down any warnings and come up with bogus reasons for why we're on the right course.
- We believe all members of the group share the same high—the *highest!*—ethical standards. We don't feel the true weight of our ethical responsibilities or the true costs and negative consequences of our behavior.
- We stereotype and discount those who question, challenge, or disagree with the group, disparaging their motives, intellect, ethics, or good faith.
- We find effective ways to pressure any group member who seems at risk for stepping off the bandwagon or questioning its direction.
- We keep ourselves in line with the group's direction, ignoring, minimizing, or explaining away our own questions, doubts, or sense of unease.
- We assure ourselves that we unanimously agree. After all, not one person has raised any serious objections or even concerns.
- Some of us guard the gates, making sure that no information or views reach the group that might call the process into question, slow the momentum, or make us rethink what we're doing.

Correspondence Bias

When we lapse into correspondence bias, which Ross (1977) called the fundamental attribution error, we see the cause of our own ethical missteps in the situation or setting, but we see that the cause of ethical missteps by other people as clearly within the individual. We were victims of circumstance; they were simply people lacking strong ethical standards, prone to seeing what they can get away with. If we fail to do the right thing in a given situation, we do it because we are overworked and exhausted, or preoccupied with a family crisis, or our boss is pressuring us, or we took the wrong dose of a new medication, or no one took the time to explain to us why we should do it another way, or it seems clear someone else will take care of it, or or or or. . . . (We rarely fail to come up with all sorts of external causes of our decisions to do the wrong thing.) But if someone else does the same thing we did in the same situation . . . What a different story! That person is ethically weak, or the kind to cut ethical corners, or basically corrupt, or, well, just a bad apple who not only should be fired from the organization, but never should have been hired in the first place. What were they thinking??? Interestingly, Western culture tends to be far more prone than other cultures to correspondence bias (Bauman & Skitka, 2010; Blanchard-Fields, Chen, Horhota, & Wang, 2007; Jones, 1979; Ross & Nisbett, 2011; Tam, Sharma, & Kim, 2016).

WYSIATI

The final treacherous tendency discussed here is perhaps the simplest, the most common, and the most easily overlooked: We too often tend to assume that we have all the information we need to understand something. Kahneman (2011) calls this the WYSIATI (What You See Is All There Is) bias. We take the information at hand and construct an account of what happened, why it happened, and what actions we need to take, if any. The less information we have, the more confidence we tend to have in the tapestry that we're weaving. We have fewer pieces of the story to fit together so we find it easier to fit them into a compelling pattern without having pieces left over that just refuse to fit. All the pieces seem to naturally fit together perfectly. Research by Kahneman and his colleagues suggests that WYSIATI makes use of all sorts of other biases to create a convincing account. For example, a fact may be completely irrelevant but rather than set it aside, we'll tend to weave it into what happened, why it happened, and what we need to do about it.

The WYSIATI bias can get an almost airtight grip on us if we're vulnerable—as almost all of us are—to a related pitfall: the narrative fallacy. Nassim Taleb (2010) describes our tendency to over-simplify and over-interpret when making the facts at hand fit into an explanation:

> The narrative fallacy addresses our limited ability to look at sequences of facts without weaving an explanation into them, or, equivalently, forcing a logical link, an *arrow of relationship*, upon them. . . . Where this propensity can go wrong is when it increases our *impression* of understanding.
>
> (p. 43) [italics in original]

We can save ourselves countless problems—and sometimes avoid needless failure—if we keep WYSIATI in mind as we gather and verify information about an organization, try to make sense of that information, create a plan for strengthening ethics in the organization and the people who make up the organization, and set about putting the plan into action. It is always worth asking:

Who have I not yet talked to?
What documents have I not yet read?
What other sources of relevant information could I be missing?
What information may have been false, incomplete, misleading, or irrelevant?
What information may have changed since I reviewed it?
What perspectives am I missing?
What might happen in the near future or on down the line that would change my understanding or plan?
What else could I be missing?

This chapter has covered only a few of the most common heuristics and other sources of trouble that can derail attempts to strengthen ethics in an organization and its members or staff. Pope and Vasquez (2016) provide coverage of additional heuristics, fallacies, and so on, in an ethical context.

References

Allison, S. T., Messick, D. M., & Goethals, G. R. (1989). On being better but not smarter than others: The Muhammad Ali effect. *Social Cognition, 7*, 275–295.

Aquino, K., Reed, A., Thau, S., & Freeman, D. (2007). A grotesque and dark beauty: How moral identity and mechanisms of moral disengagement influence cognitive and emotional reactions to war. *Journal of Experimental Social Psychology, 43*(3), 385–392.

Bacon, F. (1955). The new organon. In *Selected writings of Francis Bacon* (pp. 455–540). New York, NY: Random House. (Original work published 1620)

Bandura, A. (1990). Selective activation and disengagement of moral control. *Journal of Social Issues, 46*(1), 27–46.

Bandura, A. (2016). *Moral disengagement: How good people can do harm and feel good about themselves* [Kindle for the Mac version]. New York, NY: Worth Publishers.

Bandura, A., Caprara, G. V., Barbaranelli, C., Pastorelli, C., & Regalia, C. (2001). Sociocognitive self-regulatory mechanisms governing transgressive behavior. *Journal of Personality and Social Psychology, 80*(1), 125–135.

Bauman, C. W., & Skitka, L. J. (2010). Making attributions for behaviors: The prevalence of correspondence bias in the general population. *Basic and Applied Social Psychology, 32*(3), 269–277.

Blanchard-Fields, F., Chen, Y., Horhota, M., & Wang, M. (2007). Cultural differences in the relationship between aging and the correspondence bias. *Journals of Gerontology: Series B: Psychological Sciences and Social Sciences, 62B*(6), 362–365.

Brown, J. D. (1986). Evaluations of self and others: Self-enhancement biases in social judgments. *Social Cognition, 4*, 353–376.

Buehler, R., & Griffin, D. (2003). Planning, personality, and prediction: The role of future focus in optimistic time predictions. *Organizational Behavior and Human Decision Processes, 92*(1), 80–90.

Detert, J. R., Treviño, L. K., & Sweitzer, V. L. (2008). Moral disengagement in ethical decision making: A study of antecedents and outcomes. *Journal of Applied Psychology, 93*(2), 374–391.

Epley, N., & Dunning, D. (2000). Feeling "holier than thou": Are self-serving assessments produced by errors in self- or social prediction? *Journal of Personality and Social Psychology, 79*(6), 861–875.

Gilbey, A., & Hill, S. (2012). Confirmation bias in general aviation lost procedures. *Applied Cognitive Psychology, 26*(5), 785–795.

Heck, P. R., & Krueger, J. I. (2016). Social perception of self-enhancement bias and error. *Social Psychology, 47*, pp. 327–339.

Hess, U., Cossette, M., & Hareli, S. (2016). I and my friends are good people: The perception of incivility by self, friends and strangers. *Europe's Journal of Psychology, 12*(1), 99–114.

Hubbard, D. W. (2014). *How to measure anything: Finding the value of intangibles in business.* Hoboken, NJ: John Wiley & Sons.

Janis, I. L. (1972). *Victims of groupthink.* Boston, MA: Houghton Mifflin.

Janis, I. L. (1982a). *Groupthink: Psychological studies of policy decisions and fiascoes.* Boston: Wadsworth.

Janis, I. L. (1982b). *Stress, attitudes, and decisions.* New York, NY: Praeger.

Janis, I. L., & Mann, L. (1977). *Decision making: A psychological analysis of conflict, choice, and commitment.* New York, NY: Free Press.

Jones, E. E. (1979). The rocky road from acts to dispositions. *American Psychologist, 34*(2), 107–117.

Kahneman, D. (2011). *Thinking, fast and slow* [Kindle for the Mac version]. New York, NY: Farrar, Straus and Giroux.

Kassin, S. M., Dror, I. E., & Kukucka, J. (2013). The forensic confirmation bias: Problems, perspectives, and proposed solutions. *Journal of Applied Research in Memory and Cognition, 2*(1), 42–52.

Klein, C. T., & Helweg-Larsen, M. (2002). Perceived control and the optimistic bias: A meta-analytic review. *Psychology and Health, 17*(4), 437–446.

Knobloch-Westerwick, S., Mothes, C., Johnson, B. K., Westerwick, A., & Donsbach, W. (2015). Political online information searching in Germany and the United States: Confirmation bias, source credibility, and attitude impacts. *Journal of Communication, 65*(3), 489–511.

Kukucka, J., & Kassin, S. M. (2014). Do confessions taint perceptions of handwriting evidence? An empirical test of the forensic confirmation bias. *Law and Human Behavior, 38*(3), 256–270.

Langer, E. J. (2014). *Mindfulness* (25th anniversary ed.) [Kindle for the Mac version]. Boston, MA: Capo Press.

Lench, H. C., Smallman, R., & Berg, L. A. (2016). Moving toward a brighter future: The effects of desire on judgments about the likelihood of future events. *Motivation Science, 2*(1), 33–48.

Lilienfeld, S. O. (2015, January 3–6). *The mother of all biases: Confirmation bias in science, practice, and everyday life.* 37th Annual National Institute on the Teaching of Psychology (NITOP), St. Pete Beach, Florida, January 3–6, 2015.

MacKay, C. (2009). *Memoirs of extraordinary popular delusions and the madness of crowds.* Overland Park, KS: Digireads Publishing. (Original work published 1841.)

McAlister, A. L., Bandura, A., & Owen, S. V. (2006). Mechanisms of moral disengagement in support of military force: The impact of Sept. 11. *Journal of Social and Clinical Psychology, 25*(2), 141–165.

Meehl, P. (1977). Why I do not attend case conferences. In P. Meehl (Ed.), *Psychodiagnosis: Selected papers* (pp. 225–302). New York, NY: Norton. (Original work published 1973)

Mendel, R., Traut-Mattausch, E., Jonas, E., Leucht, S., Kane, J. M., Maino, K., & Hamann, J. (2011). Confirmation bias: Why psychiatrists stick to wrong preliminary diagnoses. *Psychological Medicine, 41*(12), 2651–2659.

Messick, D. M., Bloom, S., Boldizar, J. P., & Samuelson, C. D. (1985). Why we are fairer than others. *Journal of Experimental Social Psychology, 21*(5), 480–500.

Moore, C. (2008). Moral disengagement in processes of organizational corruption. *Journal of Business Ethics, 80*(1), 129–139.

Moore, C., Detert, J. R., Klebe Treviño, L., Baker, V. L., & Mayer, D. M. (2012). Why employees do bad things: Moral disengagement and unethical organizational behavior. *Personnel Psychology, 65*(1), 1–48.

Narayanaswami, P., Geisbush, T., Jones, L., Weiss, M., Mozaffar, T., Gronseth, G., & Rutkove, S. B. (2016). Critically re-evaluating a common technique: Accuracy, reliability, and confirmation bias of EMG. *Neurology*, *86*(3), 218–223.

Nickerson, R. S. (1998). Confirmation bias: A ubiquitous phenomenon in many guises. *Review of General Psychology*, *2*(2), 175–220.

Osofsky, M. J., Bandura, A., & Zimbardo, P. G. (2005). The role of moral disengagement in the execution process. *Law and Human Behavior*, *29*(4), 371–393.

Pope, K. S., & Vasquez, M. J. (2016). *Ethics in psychotherapy and counseling: A practical guide* (5th ed.) [Kindle for the Mac version]. New York, NY: John Wiley & Sons.

Richards, P. M., Geiger, J. A., & Tussey, C. M. (2015). The dirty dozen: 12 sources of bias in forensic neuropsychology with ways to mitigate. *Psychological Injury and Law*, *8*(4), 265–280.

Ross, L. (1977). The intuitive psychologist and his shortcomings: Distortions in the attribution process. *Advances in Experimental Social Psychology*, *10*, 173–220.

Ross, L., & Nisbett, R. E. (2011). *The person and the situation: Perspectives of social psychology* (2nd ed.). London: Pinter & Martin Publishers.

Taleb, N. N. (2010). *The black swan: The impact of the highly improbable fragility* (2nd ed.) [Kindle for the Mac version]. New York, NY: Random House.

Tam, J. L., Sharma, P., & Kim, N. (2016). Attribution of success and failure in intercultural service encounters: The moderating role of personal cultural orientations. *Journal of Services Marketing*, *30*(6), 643–658.

Tappin, B. M., & McKay, R. T. (2016). The illusion of moral superiority. *Social Psychological and Personality Science*. Retrieved from http://journals.sagepub.com/doi/10.1177/1948550616673878

Walmsley, S., & Gilbey, A. (2016). Cognitive biases in visual pilots' weather-related decision making. *Applied Cognitive Psychology*, *30*(4), 532–543.

7   Finding Moral Courage and Putting It to Work

The most informed, effective steps to strengthen ethics in organizations and the people within can succeed only if we actually take the steps. Taking action requires us to leave our cocoon as passive bystanders (a.k.a. enablers) when we come across questionable or unacceptable behavior, especially when the safety and welfare of others is at stake.

We may have to push, persuade, or force ourselves to abandon the comforting insulation and safety of "it's not my problem," "someone else will take care of this," "it's probably not as bad as it looks," "I wouldn't even know where to begin," "I just don't have time for this," or "nothing I do will make a difference." We need only a second or two to shrug and turn away. Excuses and distractions crowd in from all sides, offering easy escapes. After all, if no one else has tackled this problem, why should we be the one? And if no one else has tackled the problem, maybe everything is OK after all and I'm making a big deal out of nothing.

Both research-based interventions and organizations themselves can try to help us do the right thing when confronting these challenges. Formal programs show promise in teaching and encouraging bystanders to take action in a range of situations such as theft, sexual harassment, interpersonal or systemic racism, bullying, or sexual assault (Chiose, 2014; Coker, Bush, Follingstad, & Brancato, 2017; Guerette, Flexon, & Marquez, 2013; Kleinsasser, Jouriles, McDonald, & Rosenfield, 2015; Midgett, Doumas, Trull, & Johnson, 2017; Nelson, Dunn, & Paradies, 2011; Nickerson, Aloe, Livingston, & Feeley, 2014; Palm Reed, Hines, Armstrong, & Cameron, 2015; Salmivalli, 2014; van Bommel, van Prooijen, Elffers, & van Lange, 2014; Wonderling, 2013). Organizations can try to overcome any tendencies to silence, discredit, isolate, and punish those who criticize or question the ethical status quo, and to commit to steps in the right direction (see Chapter 5). They can adopt a proactive stance and support moral courage as a management practice (Sekerka, Bagozzi, & Charnigo, 2009).

But whatever prompting, encouragement, and support we get from outside ourselves, it always comes down to each one of us as individuals and the decisions each of us makes.

Moral Courage

Making the decision to do the right thing can depend on our willingness to scrape together—or sometimes to invent—enough moral courage to act. Mark Twain noticed that moral courage was sometimes hard to find: "It is curious—curious that physical courage should be so common in the world, and moral courage so rare" (1940, p. 69).

What is moral courage? Rossouw described it as "the resolve to act on moral convictions even when it is not comfortable or self-serving to do so" (2002, p. 414). We remain committed to the moral path even when it takes us toward risk and loss and away from comfort, safety, and self-interest.

Some risks and losses stand right out in the open, easy for us to spot. An organizational backlash that punishes acts of moral courage is not uncommon. Simola discusses a typical paradox in "the expression of moral courage in organizations, which is that although morally courageous acts are aimed at fostering collective growth, vitality, and virtue, their initial result is typically one of collective unease, preoccupation, or lapse, reflected in the social ostracism and censure of the courageous member and message" (Simola, 2016a; see also 2015, 2016b). Depending on the situation, we may risk and actually cost ourselves promotions, raises, business or professional referrals and other opportunities, our job, the respect and friendship of others, and so much else. Retaliation, retribution, and revenge can take many forms, arrive quickly or be served cold. People can have long memories.

Other risks and losses—more subtle and pernicious—can sneak up and catch us unaware. We may insulate ourselves within a tight-knit group of people who see things the same way we do and demonize those who disagree. Steven Pinker (2006) describes how humans have an unfortunate tendency to bind themselves into

coalitions, professing certain beliefs as badges of their commitment to the coalition and treating rival coalitions as intellectually unfit and morally depraved. Debates . . . can make things even worse, because when the other side fails to capitulate to one's devastating arguments, it only proves they are immune to reason . . .

As we shut ourselves in, we stop reading and listening to "the other side" and anything that conveys, let alone supports, views that challenge our own. We end up having no real idea of what those who disagree with us have said or written. Our dogmatic self-righteousness blocks us from seeing the humanity of those who disagree. We must summon the moral courage to recognize and respect that humanity. Pianalto (2012) defined moral courage as willingness to face the "risk of retaliation or punishment," but added a key requirement regarding how we respond to other people:

> I suggest that moral courage also involves a capacity to face others as moral agents, and thus in a manner that does not objectify them. . . . Without facing others as moral subjects, we risk moral cowardice on the one hand and moral fanaticism on the other.
>
> (p. 165)

Moral courage that shows readiness to face risk and loss, openness to other views, and respect for those who disagree can help transform organizations. Serrat (2010) wrote: "At its most basic, moral courage helps cultivate mindful organizational environments that, among others, off-set groupthink; mitigate hypocrisy and 'nod-and-wink' cultures; educate mechanical conformity and compliance; bridge organizational silos; and check irregularities, misconduct, injustice, and corruption" (p. 2; see also Hannah, Avolio, & Walumbwa, 2011; Osswald, Greitemeyer, Fischer, & Frey, 2010; Pope & Vasquez, 2016; Simola, 2015).

It often takes moral courage to strengthen ethics in organizations and the people within the organization—whether that involves blowing the whistle inside or outside the organization, creating and circulating a survey or other means to find out what changes might help, planning steps to bring about those changes, or taking those steps.

When We Are at Fault

Strengthening ethics in organizations demands a special kind of moral courage when we ourselves helped create the problem. Breaking News: None of us is ethically perfect. All of us have made choices we knew at the time were clearly wrong even as we scrambled furiously to convince ourselves otherwise. And for most if not all of those choices to do the wrong thing we probably grabbed a good excuse right off the rack (no tailoring needed): Everybody else does it, nobody told me it was wrong, I'm in a real hurry, no one will get hurt, it's actually a gray area, no one will notice, it's no big deal, I'll do it just this once, I'll make up for it, I've been under so much stress lately, I've done so much good that I'm due this little foible, and. . . . Have I named your favorite go-to rationalizations yet or am I listing only my own? Feel free to add to the list.

Facing up to it when we, as part of an organization, have contributed in some way to its ethical weakness or its unethical behavior is hard for any of us. It can feel almost impossible to take responsibility publicly and offer a meaningful apology. We find clever ways of ducking, shifting, or diffusing responsibility. We blame others, the situation, the timing, and anything else we can think of. We stuff what we think of as "apologies" so full of abstractions, rationalizations, conditionals, extenuations, irrelevancies, excuses, and phrases that sound as if they were written by a gaggle of attorneys until they could as well serve as insults.

Consider the imaginary case of Mr. Hypothetical, who receives an email from a coworker, asking his opinion about a new company policy. He replies to this trusted friend that he hates the policy and goes on a rant about the company officer who headed up the task force that created the policy, calling her a long string of sexist, racist, and homophobic slurs. Then he hits "send."

At least that's what Mr. Hypothetical thinks he's doing. What he's actually doing is sending his message to every person in the company directory. Soon replies, many of them outraged, begin to trickle into his inbox. The trickle becomes a flood.

What does he do? Mr. Hypothetical could send an authentic apology such as:

> I did something horrible and inexcusable: I used vicious, ignorant slurs that are never warranted and that no one ever deserves. They don't reflect on anyone but me. I am profoundly sorry and hope the people I mentioned by name will allow me to apologize to each of you individually and in person. I also hope the company will allow me to apologize to all of you as a group at our next company meeting. I assume full responsibility for what I've done and its consequences, I deeply regret what I've done, and I will try to make it up to you in other ways. I will never do anything like this again.

How likely is it that Mr. Hypothetical will send such an apology? How often have you encountered such apologies? Here are a few more typical examples of what seems to pass as an apology these days.

Those words sure do not represent who I am as a person. Those who know me know that I am not racist, sexist, or homophobic. I hope everyone will forgive this inexplicable momentary lapse.

* * *

A few minutes ago you read what was supposed to be a completely private communication to a friend. Please disregard it completely. It is regrettable that this hasty draft, which I was about to erase but accidentally sent instead, reached any eyes but mine.

* * *

It may not have been clear that the message you received, which was without the context of prior messages, was a joke, a satire of racist, sexist, and homophobic views, intended to mock those who hold such unacceptable views. I am sorry it reached your mailboxes, especially without the context of prior message, but I hope no one lacks a sense of humor and that all can appreciate satire when they read it.

* * *

I regret that I hit the wrong button on my computer and sent you a message with words that are viewed as offensive, inappropriate, and politically incorrect in a business setting. I'm sorry if anyone read them and felt offended. That was certainly never my intent.

* * *

I am extremely sorry that you received and had to read that clearly racist, sexist, and homophobic message. That kind of message and the views it represents are, frankly, evil, destructive, and unforgivable. Those words hurt people on so many levels and in so many ways. They have no place in our business or in our society. Someone hacked my email account! I promise to beef up my security to make sure hackers can no longer send out such messages, making it look like they came from me.

The resistance to offering a genuine, meaningful apology can feel like an insurmountable barrier. In a remarkable book, *When Breath Becomes Air*, Paul Kalanithi (2016) described an extremely talented surgical resident, destined for greatness except for one tragic flaw: his inability to accept responsibility and apologize when he made a mistake. After committing a catastrophic blunder, the resident pleaded with Kalanithi, asking him to find some way to avoid being fired. Kalanithi assured the resident that all he had to do was to look him right in the eye, apologize, say that he was solely responsible for what happened, and promise that he would never allow it to happen in the future. The path to keeping his job was clear and yet the resident found it impossible to follow.

> "But it was the nurse who—"
> "No. You have to be able to say it and mean it. Try again."
> "But—"
> "No. Say it."
> This went on for an hour before I knew he was doomed.
> (Kalanithi, 2016, p. 80)

One of the most profound and effective steps we can take to strengthen ethics in organizations and the individuals within the organization is to be relentlessly honest with ourselves and others in taking responsibility when we have contributed to the organization's ethical weakness or violations.

Steps Toward, Around, or Over

Finally, even if we are concerned about, committed to, and focused on taking steps to prevent questionable or objectionable practices and strengthen ethics on an individual and organizational level, our lives may be so textured with tight schedules, heavy responsibilities, and constant distractions that we miss chances to make a difference. Darley and Batson (1973) conducted an experiment showing how a lack of attention to our immediate surroundings—the here and now—can lead to missed opportunities. Princeton Theological Seminary students participated in an experiment in which they were given time to prepare a brief talk in one locale and then had to give the talk in another building. As the students walked through an alley between the buildings, each found someone pretending to be a victim in need of help—slumped over in a doorway, eyes shut, head down, unmoving. The victim coughed and groaned. Half of the students prepared a talk on the parable of the Good Samaritan, and yet many did not stop to help the victim. Those who were about to talk about the importance of acting like the Good Samaritan were no more likely to stop to help than those who were assigned to talk about another topic. To save time, some stepped over the victim rather than going around.

As we go about taking steps to make ethics stronger in organizations and the people in them, this study reminds us that a chance to make a difference can come at an inconvenient time and catch us off guard by appearing in forms we did not expect, that we can pass by it without noticing, and that we need to pay attention to what shows up unannounced at every step.

References

Chiose, S. (2014, October 31). *Male bystander intervention can help end sexual assaults, experts say.* Retrieved from the Globe & Mail website: www.theglobeandmail.com/news/national/male-bystander-intervention-is-key-to-ending-sexual-assault/article21418259/?cmpid=rss1

Coker, A. L., Bush, H. M., Follingstad, D. R., & Brancato, C. J. (2017). Frequency of guns in the households of high school seniors. *Journal of School Health, 87*(3), 153–158.

Darley, J. M., & Batson, C. D. (1973). "From Jerusalem to Jericho": A study of situational and dispositional variables in helping behavior. *Journal of Personality and Social Psychology, 27*(1), 100–108.

Guerette, R. T., Flexon, J. L., & Marquez, C. (2013). Instigating bystander intervention in the prevention of alcohol-impaired driving: Analysis of data regarding mass media campaigns. *Journal of Studies on Alcohol and Drugs, 74*(2), 205–211.

Hannah, S. T., Avolio, B. J., & Walumbwa, F. O. (2011). Relationships between authentic leadership, moral courage, and ethical and pro-social behaviors. *Business Ethics Quarterly, 21*, 555–578.

Kalanithi, P. (2016). *When breath becomes air* [Kindle for the Mac version]. New York, NY: Random House.

Kleinsasser, A., Jouriles, E. N., McDonald, R., & Rosenfield, D. (2015). An online bystander intervention program for the prevention of sexual violence. *Psychology of Violence, 5*(3), 227–235.

Midgett, A., Doumas, D. M., Trull, R., & Johnson, J. (2017). Training students who occasionally bully to be peer advocates: Is a bystander intervention effective in reducing bullying behavior? *Journal of Child and Adolescent Counseling.* Retrieved from www.tandfonline.com/doi/full/10.1080/23727810.2016.1277116

Morrison, E. W. (2014). Employee voice and silence. *Annual Review of Organizational Psychology and Organizational Behavior, 1*(1), 173–197.

Nelson, J. K., Dunn, K. M., & Paradies, Y. (2011). Bystander anti-racism: A review of the literature. *Analyses of Social Issues and Public Policy*, *11*(1), 263–284.

Nickerson, A. B., Aloe, A. M., Livingston, J. A., & Feeley, T. H. (2014). Measurement of the bystander intervention model for bullying and sexual harassment. *Journal of Adolescence, 37*, 391–400.

Osswald, S., Greitemeyer, T., Fischer, P., & Frey, D. (2010). What is moral courage? Definition, explication, and classification of a complex construct. In C. L. S. Pury & S. J. Lopez (Eds.), *The psychology of courage: Modern research on an ancient virtue* (pp. 149–164). Washington, DC: American Psychological Association.

Palm Reed, K. M., Hines, D. A., Armstrong, J. L., & Cameron, A. Y. (2015). Experimental evaluation of a bystander prevention program for sexual assault and dating violence. *Psychology of Violence, 5*(1), 95–102.

Pianalto, M. (2012). Moral courage and facing others. *International Journal of Philosophical Studies, 20*(2), 165–184.

Pinker, S. (2006, December 31). Preface to dangerous ideas. *Edge*. Retrieved from https://edge.org/ conversation/ preface-to-dangerous-ideas

Pope, K. S., & Vasquez, M. J. (2016). Chapter 10: Moral distress and moral courage. In K. S. Pope & M. J. Vasquez (Eds.), *Ethics in psychotherapy and counseling: A practical guide* (5th ed.) [Kindle for the Mac version] (pp. 65–80). New York, NY: John Wiley & Sons.

Rossouw, G. J. (2002). Three approaches to teaching business ethics. *Teaching Business Ethics, 6*(4), 411–433.

Salmivalli, C. (2014). Participant roles in bullying: How can peer bystanders be utilized in interventions? *Theory into Practice, 53*, 286–292.

Sekerka, L. E., Bagozzi, R. P., & Charnigo, R. (2009). Facing ethical challenges in the workplace: Conceptualizing and measuring professional moral courage. *Journal of Business Ethics, 89*(4), 565–579.

Serrat, O. (2010). *Moral courage in organizations*. Washington, DC: Asian Development Bank.

Simola, S. (2015). Understanding moral courage through a feminist and developmental ethic of care. *Journal of Business Ethics, 130*(1), 29–44.

Simola, S. (2016a). Fostering collective growth and vitality following acts of moral courage: A general system, relational psychodynamic perspective. *Journal of Business Ethics*. Retrieved from http://link.springer.com/ article/10.1007/s10551-016-3014-0

Simola, S. (2016b). Mentoring the morally courageous: A relational cultural perspective. *Career Development International, 21*(4), 340–354.

Twain, M. (1940). *Mark Twain in eruption: Hitherto unpublished pages about men and events*. New York, NY: Harper & Brothers.

van Bommel, M., van Prooijen, J.-W., Elffers, H., & van Lange, P. A. M. (2014). Intervene to be seen: The power of a camera in attenuating the bystander effect. *Social Psychological and Personality Science, 5*, 459–466.

Wonderling, L. (2013). *Psychological first aid and the Good Samaritan*. Baltimore, MD: Cape Foundation Publications.

Index

9/11 attacks 11, 39, 49

Abu Ghraib Prison, Iraq 12–13
acquiescence 48
American Association for the
    Advancement of Science
    (AAAS) 49
American Psychological
    Association (APA) 11–17, 24–6,
    37–9, 49–50; 1992 APA ethics
    code 37; Committee on Ethical
    Standards 25; Committee on
    Scientific and Professional Ethics
    (CSPE) 25; ethics code of 24–7,
    37–9; Ethics Office 12, 38–9
Amnesty International 13–14
andon cord 51–2
annual reports 4
Annual Retail Theft Survey 6
anonymous survey(s) 28, 40, 46, 53
apology(ies) 5, 7, 11, 32, 37, 72–4
Arrigo, Jean Maria 49; and
    AAAS Scientific Freedom and
    Responsibility Award 49
Association for Psychological
    Science (APS) 17

Bacon, Francis 61
Bagram Detention Centre,
    Afghanistan 12–13
Bandura, A. 60
Bazerman, M. 36
Bellow, Saul 36
Bennis, Warren 35, 36
Bersoff, Don 38

betrayal(s) 2, 4, 32, 34–5, 40;
    institutional betrayal trauma 35;
    trauma 35
bias *see* bias of ethical
    arrogance; confirmation
    bias; correspondence bias;
    optimistic bias;
    WYSIATI bias
bias of ethical arrogance (bias
    of illusory ethical superiority)
    59–60
blind spots, personal 2, 36
bribery 6
British Psychological Society 17
bullying 17, 69
Bush administration 16
bystanders 69

California 5, 50; compulsory
    sterilization laws 5; Freemont 50;
    State Auditor 5
campus judicial systems 7
Canadian Psychological
    Association 17
Central Intelligence Agency 13,
    14–16
cheating 2, 32
child abuse 5, 33
Chronicle of Higher Education 16
confirmation bias 61–2
correspondence bias 63–4
culture of psychological
    safety 52
culture of silence and silencing
    50, 53

For Product Safety Concerns and Information please contact our EU
representative GPSR@taylorandfrancis.com
Taylor & Francis Verlag GmbH, Kaufingerstraße 24, 80331 München, Germany

www.ingramcontent.com/pod-product-compliance
Ingram Content Group UK Ltd.
Pitfield, Milton Keynes, MK11 3LW, UK
UKHW021420080625
459435UK00011B/88